WQEIC
Learning Resources Centre

Please return the book on or before the last date shown below

WITHDRAWN

** A fine is payable for each overdue book **

Independence Educational Publishers

First published by Independence Educational Publishers

The Studio, High Green

Great Shelford

Cambridge CB22 5EG

England

© Independence 2017

Copyright

Photocopy licence

ISBN-13: 978 1 86168 767 8

Printed in Great Britain

Zenith Print Group

Contents

Introduction

PRIVACY is Volume 317 in the **ISSUES** series. The aim of the series is to offer current, diverse information about important issues in our world, from a UK perspective.

ABOUT TITLE

Privacy is a fundamental human right. But is our privacy increasingly under threat? This book examines what privacy means and why it is important. It also looks at the controversial 'Snooper's Charter', data privacy, hackers and the rise of wearable technology. Also explored are issues surrounding surveillance, the rules regarding CCTV and the ethics of DNA databases. The third and final chapter looks at privacy in relation to The Internet of Things, including how your Smart TV could be spying on you and whether it's a breach of children's privacy when their parents post baby pictures on social media.

OUR SOURCES

Titles in the **ISSUES** series are designed to function as educational resource books, providing a balanced overview of a specific subject.

The information in our books is comprised of facts, articles and opinions from many different sources, including:

⇨ Newspaper reports and opinion pieces

⇨ Website factsheets

⇨ Magazine and journal articles

⇨ Statistics and surveys

⇨ Government reports

⇨ Literature from special interest groups.

A NOTE ON CRITICAL EVALUATION

Because the information reprinted here is from a number of different sources, readers should bear in mind the origin of the text and whether the source is likely to have a particular bias when presenting information (or when conducting their research). It is hoped that, as you read about the many aspects of the issues explored in this book, you will critically evaluate the information presented.

It is important that you decide whether you are being presented with facts or opinions. Does the writer give a biased or unbiased report? If an opinion is being expressed, do you agree with the writer? Is there potential bias to the 'facts' or statistics behind an article?

ASSIGNMENTS

In the back of this book, you will find a selection of assignments designed to help you engage with the articles you have been reading and to explore your own opinions. Some tasks will take longer than others and there is a mixture of design, writing and research-based activities that you can complete alone or in a group.

FURTHER RESEARCH

At the end of each article we have listed its source and a website that you can visit if you would like to conduct your own research. Please remember to critically evaluate any sources that you consult and consider whether the information you are viewing is accurate and unbiased.

Useful weblinks

www.abouthumanrights.co.uk

www.theconversation.com

www.dontspyonus.org.uk

www.equalityhumanrights.com

www.fullfact.org

GOV.UK

www.theguardian.com

www.ibtimes.co.uk

www.ico.org.uk

www.independent.co.uk

http://www.itspublicknowledge.info

www.huffingtonpost.co.uk

www.parentzone.org.uk

www.privacyinternational.org

www.telegraph.co.uk

www.wrighthassall.co.uk

www.yougov.co.uk

What is privacy?

Privacy is a fundamental right, essential to autonomy and the protection of human dignity, serving as the foundation upon which many other human rights are built.

Privacy enables us to create barriers and manage boundaries to protect ourselves from unwarranted interference in our lives, which allows us to negotiate who we are and how we want to interact with the world around us. Privacy helps us establish boundaries to limit who has access to our bodies, places and things, as well as our communications and our information.

The rules that protect privacy give us the ability to assert our rights in the face of significant power imbalances.

As a result, privacy is an essential way we seek to protect ourselves and society against arbitrary and unjustified use of power, by reducing what can be known about us and done to us, while protecting us from others who may wish to exert control.

Privacy is essential to who we are as human beings, and we make decisions about it every single day. It gives us a space to be ourselves without judgement, allows us to think freely without discrimination, and is an important element of giving us control over who knows what about us.

Why does it matter?

In modern society, the deliberation around privacy is a debate about modern freedoms.

As we consider how we establish and protect the boundaries around the individual, and the ability of the individual to have a say in what happens to him or her, we are equally trying to decide:

⇨   the ethics of modern life;

⇨   the rules governing the conduct of commerce; and

⇨   the restraints we place upon the power of the state.

Technology has always been intertwined with this right. For instance, our capabilities to protect privacy are greater today than ever before, yet the capabilities that now exist for surveillance are without precedent.

We can now uniquely identify individuals amidst mass data sets and streams, and equally make decisions about people based on broad swathes of data. It is now possible for companies and governments to monitor every conversation we conduct, each commercial transaction we undertake, and every location we visit. These capabilities may lead to negative effects on individuals, groups and even society as it chills action, excludes and discriminates. They also affect how we think about the relationships between the individual, markets, society and the state. If the situation arises where institutions we rely upon can come to know us to such a degree so as to be able to peer into our histories, observe all our actions and predict our future actions, even greater power imbalances will emerge where individual autonomy in the face of companies, groups, and governments will effectively disappear and any deemed aberrant behaviour identified, excluded and even quashed.

Perhaps the most significant challenge to privacy is that the right can be compromised without the individual being aware. With other rights, you are aware of the interference – being detained, censored, or restrained. With other rights, you are also aware of the

transgressor – the detaining official, the censor or the police.

Increasingly, we aren't being informed about the monitoring we are placed under, and aren't equipped with the capabilities or given the opportunity to question these activities.

Secret surveillance, done sparingly in the past because of its invasiveness, lack of accountability and particular risk to democratic life, is quickly becoming the default.

Privacy International envisions a world in which privacy is protected, respected and fulfilled. Increasingly institutions are subjecting people to surveillance, and excluding us from being involved in decisions about how our lives are interfered with, our information processed, our bodies scrutinised, our possessions searched. We believe that in order for individuals to participate in the modern world, developments in laws and technologies must strengthen and not undermine the ability to freely enjoy this right.

Is privacy a right?

Privacy is a qualified, fundamental human right. The right to privacy is articulated in all of the major international and regional human rights instruments, including:

United Nations Declaration of Human Rights (UDHR) 1948, Article 12: "No one shall be subjected to arbitrary interference with his privacy, family, home or correspondence, nor to attacks upon his honour and reputation. Everyone has the right to the protection of the law against such interference or attacks."

International Covenant on Civil and Political Rights (ICCPR) 1966, Article 17: "1. No one shall be subjected to arbitrary or unlawful interference with his privacy, family, home or correspondence, nor to unlawful attacks on his honour or reputation. 2. Everyone has the right to the protection of the law against such interference or attacks."

The right to privacy is also included in:

⇨ Article 14 of the United Nations Convention on Migrant Workers;

⇨ Article 16 of the UN Convention on the Rights of the Child;

⇨ Article 10 of the African Charter on the Rights and Welfare of the Child;

⇨ Article 4 of the African Union Principles on Freedom of Expression (the right of access to information);

⇨ Article 11 of the American Convention on Human Rights;

⇨ Article 5 of the American Declaration of the Rights and Duties of Man;

⇨ Articles 16 and 21 of the Arab Charter on Human Rights;

⇨ Article 21 of the ASEAN Human Rights Declaration; and

⇨ Article 8 of the European Convention on Human Rights.

Over 130 countries have constitutional statements regarding the protection of privacy, in every region of the world.

An important element of the right to privacy is the right to protection of personal data. While the right to data protection can be inferred from the general right to privacy, some international and regional instruments also stipulate a more specific right to protection of personal data, including:

⇨ the OECD's *Guidelines on the Protection of Privacy and Transborder Flows of Personal Data*,

⇨ the Council of Europe Convention 108 for the Protection of Individuals with Regard to the Automatic Processing of Personal Data,

⇨ a number of European Union Directives and its pending Regulation, and the European Union Charter of Fundamental Rights,

⇨ the Asia-Pacific Economic Cooperation (APEC) Privacy Framework 2004, and

⇨ the Economic Community of West African States has a Supplementary Act on data protection from 2010.

Over 100 countries now have some form of privacy and data protection law.

However, it is all too common that surveillance is implemented without regard to these protections. That's one of the reasons why Privacy International is around – to make sure that the powerful institutions such as governments and corporations don't abuse laws and loopholes to invade your privacy.

⇨ The above information is reprinted with kind permission from Privacy International. Please visit www. privacyinternational.org for further information.

© *Privacy International 2017*

Support for 'snooper's charter'

Do you think that communications companies should be required to retain everyone's data – internet browsing history, emails, voice calls, social media interactions and mobile messaging – for 12 months? Police and intelligence agencies would have access to this information for anti-terrorism purposes. (%)

53% Support

31% Oppose

16% Don't know

YouGov, Jan 15–16, 2015

Article 8: respect for your private and family life

Article 8 protects your right to respect for your private life, your family life, your home and your correspondence (letters, telephone calls and emails, for example).

What is meant by private life?

You have the right to live your life privately without government interference.

The courts have interpreted the concept of 'private life' very broadly. It covers things like your right to determine your sexual orientation, your lifestyle, and the way you look and dress. It also includes your right to control who sees and touches your body. For example, this means that public authorities cannot do things like leave you undressed in a busy ward, or take a blood sample without your permission.

The concept of private life also covers your right to develop your personal identity and to forge friendships and other relationships. This includes a right to participate in essential economic, social, cultural and leisure activities. In some circumstances, public authorities may need to help you enjoy your right to a private life, including your ability to participate in society.

This right means that the media and others can be prevented from interfering in your life. It also means that personal information about you (including official records, photographs, letters, diaries and medical records) should be kept securely and not shared without your permission, except in certain circumstances.

What is meant by family life?

You have the right to enjoy family relationships without interference from government. This includes the right to live with your family and, where this is not possible, the right to regular contact.

'Family life' can include the relationship between an unmarried couple, an adopted child and the adoptive parent, and a foster parent and fostered child.

What is meant by home?

The right to respect for your home does not give you a right to housing. It is a right to enjoy your existing home peacefully. This means that public authorities should not stop you entering or living in your home without very good reason, and they should not enter without your permission. This applies whether or not you own your home.

Are there any restrictions to this right?

There are situations when public authorities can interfere with your right to respect for private and family life, home and correspondence. This is only allowed where the authority can show that its action is lawful, necessary and proportionate in order to:

⇨ protect national security

⇨ protect public safety

⇨ protect the economy

⇨ protect health or morals

⇨ prevent disorder or crime, or

⇨ protect the rights and freedoms of other people.

Action is 'proportionate' when it is appropriate and no more than necessary to address the problem concerned.

Using this right - example

A physical disabilities team at a local authority decided to use support workers to help service users enjoy social activities, including visits to pubs and clubs. But when a service user asked to be accompanied to a gay pub, the scheme manager refused on the grounds that the support workers were not prepared to attend a gay venue. Recognising the human rights angle, an advocate working on behalf of the service user challenged this decision based on the right to respect for private life.

(Example provided by the British Institute of Human Rights.)

What the law says

Article 8: right to privacy

⇨ Everyone has the right to respect for his private and family life, his home and his correspondence.

⇨ There shall be no interference by a public authority with the exercise of this right except such as is in accordance with the law and is necessary in a democratic society in the interests of national security, public safety or the economic well-being of the country, for the prevention of disorder or crime, for the protection of health or morals, or for the protection of the rights and freedoms of others.

Example case – Goodwin & I v United Kingdom [2002]

This case heard in the European Court of Human Rights explored issues for transsexual people in relation to their rights to private life and to marry. The judgement was a landmark decision for the treatment of transsexual people, a group which had not been recognised in UK law as:

⇨ their acquired gender

⇨ able to hold a birth certificate showing their acquired gender, and

⇨ able to marry someone of the opposite gender.

The Court ruled that this treatment violated both the right to private life and the right to marry. The UK Government later introduced the Gender Recognition Act 2004, creating a mechanism to enable all these things.

Last updated: 4 May 2016

⇨ The copyright in the document this publication has been adapted from and all other intellectual property rights in that material are owned by, or licensed to, the Commission for Equality and Human Rights, known as the Equality and HUman Rights Commission ("the EHRC").

Parliament passes most extreme surveillance law in UK history

The UK Parliament has passed the Investigatory Powers Bill, the most extreme surveillance law in our history.

The UK Government has failed to respond to widespread public dismay over secret mass surveillance revealed by whistleblower Edward Snowden in 2013. The Bill will not only put into statute the capabilities revealed by Snowden but extend surveillance even further.

This is not just of grave concern for UK citizens. The impact of the Bill will be felt around the world. Authoritarian leaders with poor human rights records can now point to the UK when justifying their own surveillance regimes.

The Bill will affect:

Our right to privacy: our communications, Internet use and personal data will be collected, stored and analysed, even if we are not under suspicion of a crime.

Our right to freedom of expression: freedom of expression relies on the freedom to explore and express ideas without the threat of arbitrary, unnecessary and disproportionate interference. The IP Bill will have a chilling effect on our freedom to share and discuss.

Investigative journalism: the Bill lacks sufficient guarantees for the protection of journalists and their sources. It also fails to require authorities to notify journalists before hacking into their devices.

The security of the Internet: bulk hacking powers could undermine the security of the Internet for everyone.

Intelligence sharing: the Bill fails to restrain the sharing of data and integration of technology between the UK and US.

Legal actions

A number of DSOU members are taking legal action against the UK's mass surveillance powers. The UK's legal regime for bulk surveillance is being challenged in two separate cases at the ECHR, while the data retention regime is being questioned in the UK and EU courts in the Watson (previously Watson-Davis) challenge. We expect both courts to place further demands for safeguards and restraints on the highly permissive UK surveillance regime.

Don't Spy on Us members will continue to challenge the Investigatory Powers Act and fight against mass surveillance.

Comment by Don't Spy on Us executive and affiliates

Renate Samson, Chief Executive of Big Brother Watch

"The Government's unwillingness to debate the broad spectrum of concerns voiced by members of the House of Lords, security experts, business, technologists, lawyers,

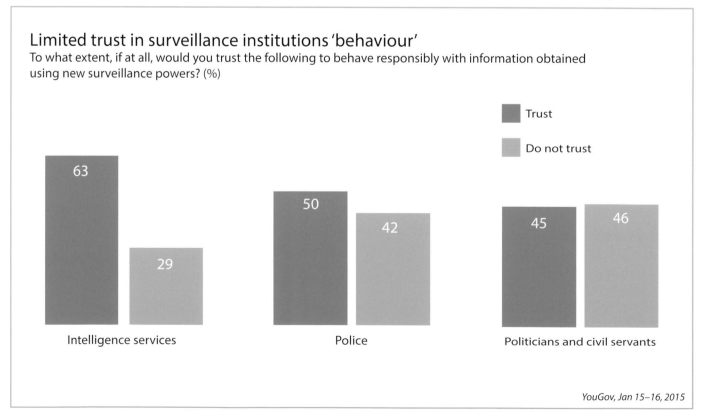

Limited trust in surveillance institutions 'behaviour'

To what extent, if at all, would you trust the following to behave responsibly with information obtained using new surveillance powers? (%)

Trust

Do not trust

Intelligence services: 63, 29

Police: 50, 42

Politicians and civil servants: 45, 46

YouGov, Jan 15–16, 2015

journalists and privacy campaigners is profoundly disappointing.

"The passing of the Investigatory Powers Bill has fundamentally changed the face of surveillance in this country; none of us online are now guaranteed the right to communicate privately and most importantly, securely."

Jo Glanville, Director of English PEN

"We know that the Snowden revelations have had a chilling effect on the free expression of journalists, writers and citizens around the world. With the passing of the Investigatory Powers Bill and its unprecedented powers to monitor our Internet use, this chill will get worse.

"The Bill fails to protect journalists and their sources and will affect investigative journalism in the UK and beyond."

Bella Sankey, Policy Director for Liberty

"The passage of the Snoopers' Charter through Parliament is a sad day for British liberty. Under the guise of counter-terrorism, the state has achieved totalitarian-style surveillance powers – the most intrusive system of any democracy in human history. It has the ability to indiscriminately hack, intercept, record and monitor the communications and Internet use of the entire population.

"Liberty has fought tooth and nail against this terrifying legislation, but the paucity of political opposition has been devastating. The fight does not end here. Our message to the Government: see you in Court."

Jim Killock, Executive Director of Open Rights Group

"The UK now has a surveillance law that is more suited to a dictatorship than a democracy. The state has unprecedented powers to monitor and analyse UK citizens' communications, regardless of whether we are suspected of any criminal activity.

"The impact of this will be felt beyond the UK's shores. It is likely that other

countries, including authoritarian regimes with poor human rights records, will use this law to justify their own intrusive surveillance powers."

Caroline Wilson Palow, General Counsel at Privacy International

"The passage of the Investigatory Powers Act is a major blow to the privacy of people in the UK and all over the world. It sets a world-leading precedent, but not one of which the Government should be proud. Instead of reining in the unregulated mass surveillance practices that have for years been conducted in secret and with questionable legal authority, the IPA now enshrines them in law. Widespread surveillance is an antithesis to democracy, yet the IPA now sanctions it. Privacy International is disappointed that Parliament has failed to curtail these broad and deep forms of surveillance that will affect each and every one of us, even if we're not suspected of any crime. But the fight is not over. It will simply move from the politicians to the judges, who will need to decide if the IPA is consistent with the rule of law and the values of our democracy."

Michelle Stanistreet, General Secretary of National Union of Journalists

"The NUJ has campaigned hard to oppose this unjustified and draconian

legislation. The secret surveillance of journalists, whistleblowers and sources is an attack on democracy and the public's right to know. The fight doesn't stop here, we will continue to stick to our ethical principles to protect journalistic sources and seek to challenge this new law in every way that is possible."

Rebecca Vincent, UK Bureau Director for Reporters Without Borders (RSF)

"Reporters Without Borders remains extremely concerned by the failure of the Investigatory Powers Bill to sufficiently protect journalists and their sources. The passage of this Bill without adequate protection mechanisms could effectively serve as a death sentence for investigative journalism in the UK. Viewed in the context of a broader trend of worrisome moves against press freedom in the UK, the adoption of this menacing Bill is very worrisome indeed."

⇨ The above information is reprinted with kind permission from Don't Spy On Us. Please visit www.dontspyonus.org.uk for further information.

© Don't Spy On Us 2017

What the Investigatory Powers Act means for you

With the passing of the Investigatory Powers Act, previously secret illegal surveillance practice revealed by Edward Snowden will now be entrenched in law, alongside new powers not used in any Western democracy. Below are some of the key ways the IPA might affect you.

Your Internet history can be logged

Every website you visit, the fact of every communication you make, and every mobile app that connects to the Internet can now be logged, recorded and made accessible to the Government.

Logs of your Internet activity, dubbed "Internet Connection Records" by the Investigatory Powers Bill doesn't already exist, and companies will be forced to spy on their customers to create the records from scratch. They are imprecisely defined, and different companies will be forced to apply the vague standards in different ways. With everything from your fridge to your car being connected online, the scope of this power, and the number of records created about your life will only grow.

Location and phone call history will be recorded

Every time you make a phone call or send a text message, your location and who you are communicating with will be logged by your mobile phone provider. This can be requested and made accessible to the Government.

The broad nature of these powers have already been struck down by the courts, but the Investigatory Powers Bill tweaks them to try and sidestep the courts' ruling.

Police will have a new data-mining super search

A new data-mining super search will allow police to combine your Internet history alongside your mobile phone location and call records as well as any other data the police may hold. No judicial warrant will be needed before the police or the intelligence agencies can use 'the filter'. Instead, the requesting body will internally authorise such access.

Your phone can be hacked even if you're not of interest

For the first time the police will be able to hack your phone, take photos using the camera, nosy through anything stored on the phone and remotely switch on the microphone – even when the phone is turned off.

Remarkably, hacking powers will be able to be used against people who "are not of intelligence interest in their own right" meaning even if you are not suspected of committing a crime of any other wrongdoing you phone could still be compromised.

The intelligence agencies will have specific powers to hack in bulk including for everyone in a particular location. While the power is intended to only be focussed outside the UK, loopholes mean it can be used at home in the UK too.

You might never be able to trust your computer again

One of the ways the police will undertake their hacking operations will be to enlist technology companies to do the hacking for them. Whether it's an app developer, Internet service provider or hardware company, the Government can now force them to assist. This means software updates pushed out to customers might be booby trapped with government backdoors.

How can you tell the difference between a backdoored software update and a legitimate one? You can't.

Your private information is less safe

Newly created massive databases to create, and store your Internet Connection Records in one place are attractive targets for cyber criminals and other attackers. The question isn't whether they will be tried to be hacked, but when.

What's worse is that companies products may not be as safe and secure as they'd like them to be. When served with a notice, companies may be forced to remove encryption which keeps data safe, or re-architect their systems to be less secure so that law enforcement can get the information they think they need. The problem is that this could weaken the security of the companies' products for every single person in the world.

Mass surveillance of communications will continue

None of the capabilities revealed during the Snowden revelations will end. Instead, they are being placed onto a legal footing so they can't be challenged as easily in the courts.

This means that on top of all the powers already listed, a further 50 billion communications events will be captured by GCHQ every single day. As there are only seven billion of us in the world, and three billion of us who have access to the Internet, the intelligence services are subjecting as many people in the world to surveillance as their computers can handle. This includes programs like Optic Nerve, which stored nude images from millions of Yahoo! webcam users.

What can you do?

Any successful campaign needs resources, whether it be for educational material, undertaking investigations, or to mount legal challenges. Any donations you are able to make to NGOs can help fight back against mass surveillance and the intrusion into your private life.

You can read up on the Bill and educate your friends and family as to the concerns and dangers. Other articles about what the IPBill means have been published by *The Guardian, the Verge, Wired*, or *Computer World* among many others.

You can help ensure that your communications are technically protected by practicing good operational security – and teaching others how to do this. There are great guides out there to get yourself up to speed or help double check what is good practice.

⇨ The above information is reprinted with kind permission from Don't Spy On Us. Please visit www.dontspyonus.org.uk for further information.

What is the Snooper's Charter and should you be worried? Here's everything you need to know

The Investigatory Powers Bill will be signed into UK law later this year, but what is it?

By Jason Murdock

The Investigatory Powers Bill – dubbed the Snooper's Charter by critics – will be signed into UK law by the end of 2016. It will enhance the spying powers open to police, intelligence agencies and public bodies and will provide strong legal backing for "bulk" collection (and hacking) of communications.

That means metadata about your phone calls, text messages, Internet browsing histories, voice-call records and social media conversations will be stored by communications providers for at least 12 months and handed over to law enforcement and security services upon request.

It also will result in bulk interception of communications, bulk hacking and the collection of bulk personal datasets being given legal backing. Essentially, it legalises the slew of spy programs that have been used by GCHQ, MI5 and MI6 for years without parliamentary oversight.

The proposals, spearheaded by current UK Prime Minister Theresa May, aim to bring together a number of separate and outdated laws – including the Regulation of Investigatory Powers Act and the Telecommunications Act 1984 – under one piece of central legislation.

Yet the proposals have been roundly criticised by technology firms, human rights groups and even internal government groups. The UK's own Intelligence Committee said the Bill was rushed and lacked clarity. The Open Rights Group said the proposals were "draconian". Privacy International said it signified a "grim watershed moment" for personal privacy.

Bulk collection and interception

One of the most shocking aspects of the Snowden disclosures from 2013 was the sheer amount of information being collected in bulk by security agencies, including the National Security Agency (NSA) and Government Communications Headquarters (GCHQ). Outed spy programs, including Prism, XKeyscore and Tempora, we discovered, allow spies to sift through vast amounts of communications data.

The Investigatory Powers Bill aims to legalise most of this bulk collection of phone records, web data and personal messages – be it email or text. In each case, "metadata" will be retained – this is the "who, when, where and how" info of a communication but not its content.

The Bill features both bulk interception and bulk collection. The first involves "intercepting international communications as they travel across networks" and the second is data that is "obtained from communications service providers".

If the collection of metadata and not content appears to be a welcome compromise, think again. Metadata "can reveal a lot more about the content of your calls than the Government is implying," the Electronic Freedom Foundation (EFF) claims, adding that it "provides enough context to know some of the most intimate details of your lives".

Internet records

The collection of Internet data – Internet connection records (ICRs) in the Bill – will be opened up to the police and intelligence services. They will be stored by Internet providers – think TalkTalk, Virgin or BT – for at least a year and will include metadata, such as when you visited a website, at what time and from what computer.

In short, ICRs will list all your Internet activity. Every website you visit and smartphone app you access. According to Big Brother Watch, the collection of this content "can reveal more about us than we realise".

It said: "They can reveal our health and finances, our sexuality, race, religion, age, location, family, friends and work connections. They can also reveal our internal thoughts, anxieties and desires, information we won't even share with the people we trust the most."

Hacking powers

Agencies like GCHQ and MI6 will be given legal authority to hack into targeted computer systems as part of investigations. Called "equipment interference" in the Investigatory Powers Bill, it warrants both physical hacking (downloading data from a device in procession) and covert interference (extracting data remotely).

"At the lower end of the scale, an equipment interference agency may covertly download data from a subject's mobile device when it is left unattended, or an agency may use someone's login credentials to gain access to data held on a computer," states the Code of Practice. "More complex equipment interference operations may involve exploiting existing vulnerabilities in software in order to gain control of devices or networks to remotely extract material or monitor the user of the device."

"We question whether hacking can ever be a legitimate form of state surveillance," said Privacy International. "The logging of keystrokes, tracking of locations, covert photography and video recording of the user and those around them enables intelligence agencies and the police to conduct real-time surveillance."

Bulk personal datasets

Bulk personal datasets (BPD), often overlooked, include banking data, travel information, passport scans, medical documentation and hospital records "about a wide range of individuals, the majority of whom are not of direct intelligence interest." In many cases, they are "too large to be manually processed".

Conservative MP David Davis previously told the UK joint committee: "This is very intrusive information for a state to hold. We are pretty sure they have all the communications data, they have got flight data, they have almost certainly got financial data, and they may well have Automatic Number Plate Recognition data."

MI5 argues that BPDs – stored in searchable databases – are used to "understand a subject of interest's behaviour and connections, and to quickly exclude the innocent". Critics point out that for this approach to work, everything has to be collected on a massive scale, leading to very real privacy concerns.

Oversight

The Government maintains that Parliament will have greater oversight than ever before – however, to be fair, the bar was fairly low to begin with. In March this year, Theresa May claimed the Bill had been changed to strengthen the powers of an oversight commissioner and to introduce enhanced safeguards around interception warrants.

"The commissioner will have a clear mandate to inform Parliament and the public about the need for, and use of, investigatory powers. The commissioner will report publicly and make recommendations on the findings that emerge in the course of his or her work," the UK Government has said. Additionally, the updated system boasts a so-called "double-lock" on warrant authorisation, alongside the need for the prime minister to be consulted before the interception of particularly sensitive communications.

In August, a 200-page report was released by David Anderson QC, the UK's former Independent Reviewer of Terrorism Legislation, which effectively green-lit the bulk surveillance proposals. He concluded there was "no viable alternative" to the current spying regime.

With current surveillance legislation – the Data Retention and Investigatory Powers Act 2014 – set to expire on 31 December this year, the Investigatory Powers Bill is now expected to gain Royal Assent and be signed into law well in advance of that date.

What does the future hold?

"The passing of the IP Bill will have an impact that goes beyond the UK's shores," said Jim Killock, executive director of the Open Rights Group. "It is likely that other countries, including authoritarian regimes with poor human rights records, will use this law to justify their own intrusive surveillance powers.

"While parliamentarians have failed to limit these powers, the courts may succeed," he continued. "A ruling by the Court of Justice of the European Union, expected next year, may mean that parts of the Bill are shown to be unlawful and need to be amended."

Meanwhile, Paul Bernal, a leading privacy and human rights expert, told IBTimes UK the introduction of the surveillance law could be "easily misused" by future governments and unexpected political change.

"The rapidity of recent political change, from Brexit to the election of Trump, should alert us to the danger," he said. "These powers are actually better suited for monitoring and controlling political dissent than catching criminals and terrorists – they're ideal for an authoritarian clampdown should a government wish to do that. A future government might well."

23 November 2016

⇨ The above information is reprinted with kind permission from the *International Business Times*. Please visit www.ibtimes. co.uk for further information.

Data Privacy Day: what it is and why we need to be more aware

Data protection needs priority in our lives right now.

By Agamoni Ghosh

In the digital age, it becomes imperative for us to protect our privacy, especially our personal data on devices and social media sites. To raise awareness on the importance of data protection, United States, Canada, India and 47 European countries are commemorating Data Privacy Day on Saturday.

IBTimes UK tells you all you need know about the day:

When is it and why is it commemorated?

Marked as an international holiday, 28 January, is widely recognised as Data Privacy Day or Data Protection Day to raise awareness and promote privacy and data protection practices.

History

The first ever legally-binding international treaty dealing with privacy and data protection was the signing of Convention 108 on 28 January, 1981 by the Council of Europe. Years later, Data Privacy Day was initiated by the Council in 2007. Two years later, in 2009 the United States House of Representatives recognised National Data Privacy Day and the United States Senate recognised Data Privacy Day in 2010 and 2011.

It has continued through the efforts of various groups and organisations since.

Some of the major participating organisations are:

⇨ Federal Trade Commission (FTC)

⇨ Federal Communication Commission (FCC)

⇨ Federal Bureau of Investigation (FBI)

⇨ Identity Theft Council

⇨ Anti-Phishing Working Group

⇨ Cyber Data-Risk Managers

⇨ EDUCAUSE.

Why should you care?

Cybersecurity is the biggest concern across all governments right now, from people's personal data being stolen to financial institutions losing billions in cyber heists. CSO (Central Statistics Office) estimates that cybercrime damage costs will hit $6 trillion annually by 2021.

In UK, hacking attempts on businesses have grown rapidly with insurance claims for data breach being made at a rate of more than one per day. Various studies show businesses, in particular, are mostly unaware of breaches that take place and even when they do, it's often too late. The Yahoo hack is the best example, where personal credentials of over 1.5 billion people were accessed by suspected state-sponsored hackers.

From your personal email account to the election ballot of a country like the US, everything can be hacked. While it is tough to fend off such huge attacks, on a personal level we need to be aware. Passwords need to be stronger, public WiFi usage needs to be limited and more money needs to be spent on antivirus software. Microsoft estimates that by 2020, almost four billion people will be online, which makes their data even more vulnerable.

28 January 2017

⇨ The above information is reprinted with kind permission from the *International Business Times*. Please visit www.ibtimes.co.uk for further information.

© *International Business Times 2017*

Sir Tim Berners-Lee slams internet's evolution and risks it poses to privacy

Sir Tim is frustrated with pernicious ads and privacy violations

By Josie Cox

Sir Tim Berners-Lee, the man credited with inventing the World Wide Web, has given a series of interviews in which he has criticised how the Internet has developed, condemned how advertising has evolved and warned of the risks that global connectivity poses to users' privacy.

In an interview with *The Guardian*, Sir Tim said that the Trump administration's decision to allow internet service providers to sign away their customers' privacy and sell users' browsing habits is "disgusting" and "appalling".

The problem with the Internet, he said, is that it can be "ridiculously revealing".

"You have the right to go to a doctor in privacy where it's just between you and the doctor. And similarly, you have to be able to go to the Web."

He also launched criticism at the way in which the Internet is used for so-called "clickbait" journalism.

"Clickbait, which is written in such a seductive way that it's almost impossible not to click on it, along with pop-up advertising, are both pushing people very, very hard so that they're liable to lash back and just deliberately pay for anything that won't have ads, basically," he said.

In a separate interview, he told *Wired UK* that online privacy should be a human right but is being "trampled on".

"You can't mess with human rights like that without massive unexpected and very disastrous consequences," he was quoted as saying.

Speaking to *MIT Technology Review*, Sir Tim said that the Internet's "social networks should be thinking about how they can tweak their systems to make truth more likely to propagate, and fake news likely to fade out".

Sir Tim, a Professor at Massachusetts Institute of Technology and the University of Oxford, was this week awarded the Association for Computing Machinery's Turing Award, which is often referred to as the Nobel Prize of Computing and carries prize money of $1 million.

He is credited with creating the World Wide Web in 1989 while working at CERN, the European Organization for Nuclear Research, and ACM said that it was this week honouring him because of the Internet's "contribution of lasting and major technical importance to the computing community, due to its simplicity, elegance and extensibility".

"It is hard to imagine the world before Sir Tim Berners-Lee's invention," said ACM President Vicki Hanson. "In many ways, the colossal impact of the World Wide Web is obvious. Many people, however, may not fully appreciate the underlying technical contributions that make the Web possible."

5 April 2017

⇨ The above information is reprinted with kind permission from *The Independent*. Please visit www.independent.co.uk for further information.

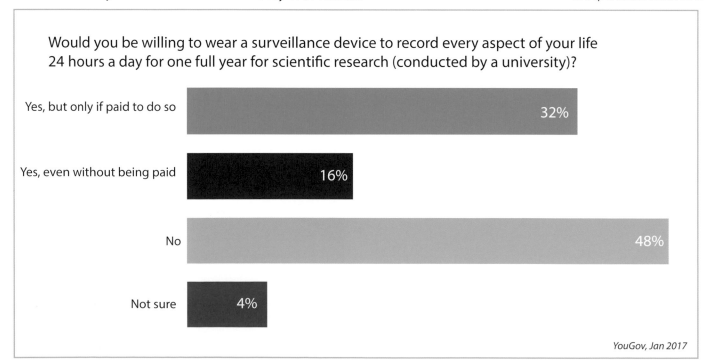

Would you be willing to wear a surveillance device to record every aspect of your life 24 hours a day for one full year for scientific research (conducted by a university)?

- Yes, but only if paid to do so — 32%
- Yes, even without being paid — 16%
- No — 48%
- Not sure — 4%

YouGov, Jan 2017

Hackers can guess your PIN just using the motion sensor on your phone

It's not just your PIN, passwords too.

By Tom White and Thomas Tamblyn

So here's some worrying news: hackers can actually find out your PIN and passwords just by analysing the way you tilt a phone in your hand.

The revelation comes from cyber experts at Newcastle University who say they've developed a technique which allows them to easily monitor the motion sensors on smartphones and tablets.

By detecting the movement of a device while the keyboard is being used the team say they were able to crack a four-digit PIN with 70% accuracy on the first guess and then with 100% accuracy by the fifth.

Lead author Dr Maryam Mehrnezhad, a research fellow in the School of Computing Science, said: "Most smartphones, tablets and other wearables are now equipped with a multitude of sensors, from the well-known GPS, camera and microphone to instruments such as the gyroscope, rotation sensors and accelerometer.

"But because mobile apps and websites don't need to ask permission to access most of them, malicious programs can covertly 'listen in' on your sensor data and use it to discover a wide range of sensitive information about you, such as phone call timing, physical activities and even your touch actions, PINs and passwords."

Because there is no uniform way of managing sensors across the industry, the research points towards there being a real threat to personal security.

Yet despite these findings the authors believe that many of the major companies involved have yet to find a way to tackle this problem, even though they're fully aware that they exist.

After publishing the findings today in the *International Journal of Information Security*, the team is now looking at the additional risks posed by personal

fitness trackers which are linked to online profiles.

Dr Mehrnezhad said: "More worryingly on some browsers we found that if you open a page on your phone or tablet which hosts one of these malicious codes and then open, for example, your online banking account without closing the previous tab, then they can spy on every personal detail you enter.

"And worse still, in some cases, unless you close them down completely, they can even spy on you when your phone is locked.

"Despite the very real risks, when we asked people which sensors they were most concerned about we found a direct correlation between perceived risk and understanding.

"So people were far more concerned about the camera and GPS than they were about the silent sensors."

The team was able to identify 25 different sensors which came as

standard on most smart devices and were used to give different information about the device and its user.

The researchers found that each user touch action – clicking, scrolling, holding and tapping – induced a unique orientation and motion trace and so on a known webpage, the team was able to determine what part of the page the user was clicking on and what they were typing.

They said they had alerted all the major browser providers such as Google and Apple of the risks but so far no-one has been able to come up with an answer.

⇨ The above information is reprinted with kind permission from the Press Association. Please visit www.pressassociation.com for further information.

© Press Association 2017

Freedom of Information (FOI): at a glance

FOI gives you a right to receive information

FOI applies to public authorities

The FOI right covers recorded information

Your request must be made in writing (by letter or email)

Public authorities must help you – it's their duty

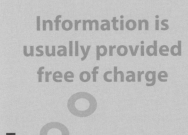

In you want environmental information different rules apply

Authorities must respond within 20 working days

Information is usually provided free of charge

Information can only be witheld if the law allows it

If you're unhappy you can appeal

Contact the Commissioner for information and advice

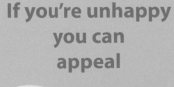

Most requests result in the information being provided

Source: Scottish Information Commissioner, itspublicknowledge.info

Privacy and the online world in 2016

Predictions for the hot talking points for 2016 regarding families and the internet.

By Geraldine Bedell, Parent Zone editorial director

Just before Christmas, the EU passed new regulations concerning online privacy. The text still has to be approved and won't become official for another couple of years – but the regulations mean, for example, that companies won't be able to pass on information they've collected about users to a third party without the user's permission. (If, like me, you're a cynic, expect your T&Cs to become even more opaque.)

Tucked in among the new regs was one saying that social media sites must increase the age at which young people can access their services without their parents' permission, from 13 to 16. Cue an outcry from tech companies, alarmed by the costs of policing this (you won't find them saying so, but they can't keep under-13s off as it is) and from child protection bodies, worried that young people will be barred from accessing helpful information; for example, about sexuality or their rights.

Whether or not you think it's right that parents should control under-16s' Internet access (and we probably don't even agree about it in the Parent Zone office, where we think about it all the time) it doesn't matter in the UK at the moment: the EU responded to the backlash by deciding at the last minute that member states could choose whether to implement this particular rule. The UK has already said it will be sticking with things as they are.

But the row did expose privacy as a raw issue, with many different groups fighting over the rights and wrongs of collecting and passing on users' (especially children's) data. Data collection is fundamental to the business model of the Internet and it would be idiotic to pretend otherwise. In practice, most of us decide (perhaps after thinking about it carefully, perhaps not) that the benefits of the online services we use are worth giving up our data for.

But things are about to change, literally. We are seeing the beginning of the Internet of things, when all sorts of household objects will be able to collect information about us. In 2015 there was an outcry when it was reported that Samsung smart TVs "could be spying on their owners" whose "spoken words could be captured and transmitted to a third party." I, for one, don't particularly want my (very) occasional episodes of ratty, bad-tempered parenting reported by my kettle.

Samsung pointed out that the televisions were simply learning from voice commands and, besides, the listening-in option could be turned off – but you can see how this could become an issue for families, opening up an Orwellian prospect of their comings and goings, their fights and make ups, becoming public property.

So, this year, expect lots of debate about blocking software (again). Also, discussion about whether anyone will ever again achieve privacy and anonymity in the world of the Internet of things or whether the latest technology will always outsmart us. Plus there will be lots of talk about the need for corporations to become more transparent. Why shouldn't tech companies tell us who is collecting our data, what they're interested in, who they're sharing it with and what are those others doing with it?

What companies do with our data is only one part of the privacy question. There are also new possibilities for hacking. One hacker group last year arranged for a brand of talking doll to start swearing – which is quite funny unless it happened to be your child's doll. But what if a much less benign group decided to hack the NHS, or your car when you were on the motorway?

As the Edward Snowden revelations showed, governments can't be trusted not to snoop on citizens – so while the EU is protecting us from companies, it's reasonable to ask what new information governments are now able to find out about us.

One way and another, privacy is going to be a major issue of concern for 2016 – and because we find it easier to focus on how these issues relate to children, and because children are a special case, requiring extra protection, much of this will be seen through the prism of the family. The rights of parents, the state and corporations will clash over children's online lives.

⇨ The above information is reprinted with kind permission from Parent Zone. Please visit www.parentzone.org.uk for further information.

© Parent Zone 2017

Can the boss now read your messages at work?

Claim

A court decision gives employers the right to check all the messages an employee sends from company computers.

Conclusion

The decision was that privacy rights don't rule out employers checking whether staff are sending personal messages on work computers, in particular circumstances. It doesn't directly change UK law, which already allows some monitoring.

On 12 January, the European Court of Human Rights decided that the employers of a Romanian man who checked messages he'd sent at work hadn't violated his right to privacy.

It's not obvious that this makes an immediate difference to employees at their desks in Blighty.

Sacked for sending personal messages at work

In 2007, Bogdan Bărbulescu's Yahoo Messenger account was examined by his bosses to check his claim that he hadn't used it for personal purposes – which was against the company's rules.

He was sacked, challenged this in the courts of Romania, and lost. He then took his argument to the human rights court in Strasbourg.

Those judges concluded that "it is not unreasonable for an employer to want to verify that the employees are completing their professional tasks during working hours".

They said that it wasn't the content of the messages that led to the employee's dismissal. It was the fact that they weren't about work that was Mr Bărbulescu's undoing.

Does the verdict change the law in this country?

The BBC originally reported that decisions of the human rights court "binds all countries that have ratified the European Convention on Human Rights, which includes Britain".

But the Convention says that countries "undertake to abide by the final judgment of the Court *in any case to which they are parties*" (our emphasis).

The only country that was a "party" to this case was Romania. It's bound to follow the court's decision (which in this case involves doing nothing, as

the human rights judges agreed with the Romanian courts).

The UK's Human Rights Act says that judgments of the human rights court must be taken into account by our courts. This isn't quite the same as them being legally binding in this country.

Things would have been different if this were a ruling from the European Union Court of Justice, as EU law trumps UK law if there is a conflict. The human rights court isn't an EU body. It's part of the Council of Europe, which has 47 members to the EU's 28.

This particular case might be unusual

British judges might still be influenced by this decision. Experts disagree, as they often do, about its importance.

Court decisions may be of immediate importance or significance down the line. They may simply be in line with what judges have said before.

Sometimes a case sets a precedent that would be followed if that exact situation came up again, but won't necessarily be followed if the facts are merely similar.

For example, the human rights court said in Mr Bărbulescu's case that "his complaint before the Court is limited to the monitoring of his communications within the framework of disciplinary proceedings".

It also noted that "the employer's monitoring was limited in scope and proportionate".

There was no violation of privacy rights in these circumstances. That doesn't mean that blanket surveillance when there's no particular reason to do so would be acceptable.

The judges also stressed that personal use of office computers were specifically forbidden by Mr Bărbulescu's firm. This made the case different from previous ones where employees were successful in their privacy complaint. In those cases, the personal use of office facilities was "allowed or, at least, tolerated".

One of the seven judges came to a different conclusion on the case, partly because he disagreed that this was relevant. He said that the ban on personal communications didn't mention "an Internet surveillance policy being implemented in the workplace". But the other six overruled him.

Finally, the court noted that Mr Bărbulescu had stated in writing that his account contained only messages about work. Taking him at his word, his employer wouldn't have expected to find any sensitive personal information when it looked at his account.

Again, if this weren't the case, judges might take a different view.

Should I be worried about being watched in the office?

An employment law specialist at the technology and digital media law firm Kemp Little told us that the outcome of Mr Bărbulescu's case "is actually broadly in line with existing English Employment Tribunal decisions in this area".

The official UK Government website already tells readers that "employers might monitor workers. This could be done in various ways, like… checking a worker's emails or the websites they look at".

The conciliation service Acas advises that employers might keep an eye on "excessive private use of emails, Internet use, etc", but that workers should be told about it.

As our legal advisor, Joshua Rozenberg, said on BBC's *PM* programme last night, employees worried about being monitored should check their contract. If it or company policy bans you from using work computers to send personal messages, you're less likely to be able to plead privacy.

14 January 2016

⇨ The above information is reprinted with kind permission from Full Fact. Please visit www.fullfact.org for further information.

Why the rise of wearable tech to monitor employees is worrying   THE CONVERSATION

An article from The Conversation.

By Ivan Manokha, Departmental Lecturer in International Political Economy, University of Oxford

An increasing number of companies are beginning to digitally monitor their employees. While employers have always scrutinised their workers' performance, the rise of wearable technology to keep tabs has more of a dystopian edge to it. Monitoring has become easier, more intrusive and is not just limited to the workplace – it's 24/7.

Devices such as Fitbit, Nike+ FuelBand and Jawbone UP, which can record information related to health, fitness, sleep quality, fatigue levels and location, are now being used by employers who integrate wearable devices into employee wellness programmes.

One of the first was BP America, which introduced Fitbit bracelets in 2013. In 2015 at least 24,500 BPs employees were using them and more and more US employers have followed suit. For instance, the same year, Vista Staffing Solutions, a healthcare recruitment agency, started a weight-loss programme using Fitbits and WiFi-enabled bathroom scales. Appirio, a consulting company, started handing out Fitbits to employees in 2014.

In the UK, similar projects are under consideration by major employers. And this trend will only intensify in the years to come. By 2018, estimates suggest that more than 13 million of these devices will be part of worker wellness schemes. Some analysts say that by the same year, at least 2 million employees worldwide will be required to wear health-and-fitness trackers as a condition of employment.

According to some, this is a positive development. Chris Brauer, an academic at Goldsmiths, University of London, argues that corporate managers will now be comparable to football managers. They will be equipped with a dashboard of employee performance trajectories, as well as their fatigue and sleep levels. They will be able to pick only the fittest employees for important business meetings, presentations, or negotiations.

It seems, however, that such optimism overlooks important negative and potentially dangerous social consequences of using this kind of technology. History here offers a word of warning.

Historical precedent

The monitoring of workers' health outside the workplace was once attempted by the Ford Motor Company. When Ford introduced a moving assembly line in 1913 – a revolutionary innovation that enabled complete control over the pace of work – the increase in productivity was dramatic. But so was the rise in worker turnover. In 1913, every time the company wanted to add 100 men to its factory personnel, it was necessary to hire 963, as workers struggled to keep up with the pace and left shortly after being recruited.

Ford's solution to this problem was to double wages. In 1914, the introduction of a US$5 a day wage was announced, which immediately led to a decline in worker turnover. But high wages came with a condition: the adoption of healthy and moral lifestyles.

The company set up a sociology department to monitor workers' – and their families' – compliance with its standards. Investigators would make unannounced calls upon employees and their neighbours to gather information on living conditions and lifestyles. Those that were deemed insufficiently healthy or morally right were immediately disqualified from the US$5 wage level.

Analysing Ford's policies, Italian political philosopher and revolutionary

Antonio Gramsci coined the term "Fordism" for this social phenomenon. It signalled fundamental changes to labour, which became much more intense after automation. Monitoring workers' private lives to control their health, Gramsci argued, was necessary to preserve "a certain psycho-physical equilibrium which prevents the physiological collapse of the worker, exhausted by the new method of production".

Parallels today

Today, we are faced with another great change to how work is done. To begin with, the "great doubling" of the global labour force has led to the increase in competition between workers around the world. This has resulted in a deterioration of working and employment conditions, the growth of informal and precarious labour, and the intensification of exploitation in the West.

So there has been a significant increase in the average number of hours worked and an increase in the intensity of labour. For example, research carried out by the Trade Union Congress in 2015 discovered that the number of people working more than 48 hours in a week in the UK was rising and it warned of a risk of "burnout Britain".

Indeed, employee burnouts have become a major concern of employers. A UK survey of human resources directors carried out in 2015 established that 80% were afraid of losing top employees to burnout.

Ford's sociology department was shut down in the early 1920s for two reasons. It became too costly to maintain it in the context of increasing competition from other car manufacturers. And also because of growing employee resistance to home visits by inspectors, increasingly seen as too intrusive into their private lives.

Wearable technology, however, does not suffer from these inconveniences. It is not costly and it is much less obviously intrusive than surprise home visits by company inspectors. Employee resistance appears to be low, though there have been a few attempts to fake the results of the tracking (for example, workers strapping their employer-provided Fitbits onto their dogs to boost their 'activity levels'). The idea of being tracked has mostly gone unchallenged.

Labour commodified to the extreme

But the use of wearable technology by employers raises a range of concerns. The most obvious is the right to privacy. The use of wearable technology goes significantly further

than computer systems where emails are already logged and accessible to employers.

Surveillance becomes continuous and all-encompassing, increasingly unconfined to the workplace, and also constitutes a form of surveillance which penetrates the human body. The right to equal employment opportunities and promotion may also be compromised if employers reserve promotion for those who are in a better physical shape or suffer less from fatigue or stress.

It may also be argued that the use of wearable technology takes what the Hungarian historian Karl Polanyi called the "commodification" of human labour to an extreme. Monitoring worker health both inside and outside the workplace involves the treatment of people as machines whose performance is to be maximised at all costs. However, as Polanyi warned, human labour is a "fictitious commodity" – it is not "produced" for sale to capital as a mere tool. To treat it as such risks ultimately leading to a "demolition of society".

To protect individual rights, systems have been introduced to regulate how data that is gathered on employees is stored and used. So one possible solution is to render the data collected by trackers compulsorily anonymous. For example, one company that collects and monitors employee data for companies, Sociometric Solutions, only charts broader patterns and connections to productivity, rather than individual performance.

This, however, does not address concerns about the increasing commodification of human labour that comes with the use of wearable technology and any potential threats to society. To prevent this, it is perhaps necessary to consider imposing an outright ban on its use by employers altogether.

3 January 2016

⇨ The above information is reprinted with kind permission from *The Conversation*. Please visit www.theconversation.com for further information.

How to delete yourself (and your searches) from Google's memory

By Thomas Tamblyn

Your Google account is a powerful tool. Through tracking and artificial intelligence it helps shapes Gmail, Google Maps and YouTube into the service that you see today.

There is however a downside to all of this, and that is that to do all that Google tracks pretty much every action you take within its services.

So if you play a YouTube video, search for an image or translate a piece of text Google keeps a record of everything.

If this, rather understandably, fills you with dread then don't panic. The company has released a website called My Activity which shows in detail your activity through Google's many services.

That includes every search you've ever made, every YouTube video you've ever watched and more.

Now if that worries you then don't panic because My Activity was created to give you control over all of this.

You can now login, review and delete these activities individually giving you far more control over your online activity and Google's tracking of it.

8 July 2016

⇨ The above information is reprinted with kind permission from The Huffington Post UK. Please visit www.huffingtonpost.co.uk for further information.

Data surveillance is all around us, and it's going to change our behaviour

An article from **The Conversation.**

THE CONVERSATION

By Uri Gal, Associate Professor in Business Information Systems, University of Sydney

Enabled by exponential technological advancements in data storage, transmission and analysis, the drive to "datify" our lives is creating an ultra-transparent world where we are never free from being under surveillance.

Increasing aspects of our lives are now recorded as digital data that are systematically stored, aggregated, analysed and sold. Despite the promise of big data to improve our lives, all encompassing data surveillance constitutes a new form of power that poses a risk not only to our privacy, but to our free will.

Data surveillance started out with online behaviour tracking designed to help marketers customise their messages and offerings. Driven by companies aiming to provide personalised product, service and content recommendations, data were utilised to generate value for customers.

But data surveillance has become increasingly invasive and its scope has broadened with the proliferation of the internet-of-things and embedded computing. The former expands surveillance to our homes, cars and daily activities by harvesting data from smart and mobile devices. The latter extends surveillance and places it inside our bodies where biometric data can be collected.

Two characteristics of data surveillance enable its expansion.

It's multifaceted

Data are used to track and circumscribe people's behaviour across space and time dimensions. An example of space-based tracking is geo-marketing. With access to real-time physical location data, marketers can send tailored ads to consumers' mobile devices to prompt them to visit stores in their vicinity. To maximise their effectiveness, marketers can tailor the content and timing of ads based on consumers' past and current location behaviours, sometimes without consumers' consent.

Location data from GPS or street maps can only approximate a person's location. But with recent technology, marketers can accurately determine whether a consumer has been inside a store or merely passed by it. This way they can check whether serving ads has resulted in a store visit, and refine subsequent ads.

Health applications track and structure people's time. They allow users to plan daily activities, schedule workouts, and monitor their progress. Some applications enable users to plan their caloric intake over time. Other applications let users track their sleep pattern.

While users can set their initial health goals, many applications rely on the initial information to structure a progress plan that includes recommended rest times, workout load, caloric intake and sleep. Applications can send users notifications to ensure compliance with the plan: a reminder that a workout is overdue; a warning that a caloric limit is reached; or a positive reinforcement when a goal has been reached. Despite the sensitive nature of these data, it is not uncommon that they are sold to third parties.

It's opaque and distributed

Our digital traces are collected by multiple governmental and business entities which engage in data exchange through markets whose structure is mostly hidden from people.

Data are typically classified into three categories: first-party, which companies gather directly from their customers through their website, app, or customer-relationship-management system; second-party, which is another company's first-party data and is acquired directly from it; and third-party, which is collected, aggregated and sold by specialised data vendors.

Despite the size of this market, how data are exchanged through it remains unknown to most people (how many of us know who can see our Facebook likes, Google searches or Uber rides, and what they use these data for?).

Some data surveillance applications go beyond recording to predicting behavioural trends.

Predictive analytics are used in healthcare, public policy and management to render organisations and people more productive. Growing

in popularity, these practices have raised serious ethical concerns around social inequality, social discrimination and privacy. They have also sparked a debate about what predictive big data can be used for.

It's nudging us

A more worrying trend is the use of big data to manipulate human behaviour at scale by incentivising 'appropriate' activities, and penalising "inappropriate" activities. In recent years, governments in the UK, US, and Australia have been experimenting with attempts to 'correct' the behaviour of their citizens through 'nudge units'.

With the application of big data, the scope of such efforts can be greatly extended. For instance, based on data acquired (directly or indirectly) from your favourite health app, your insurance company could raise your rates if it determined your lifestyle to be unhealthy. Based on the same data, your bank could classify you as a 'high-risk customer' and charge you a higher interest on your loan.

Using data from your smart car, your car insurance company could decrease your premium if it deemed your driving to be safe.

By signalling "appropriate behaviours" companies and governments aim to

shape our behaviour. As the scope of data surveillance increases, more of our behaviours will be evaluated and "corrected" and this disciplinary drive will become increasingly inescapable.

With this disciplinary drive becoming routine, there is a danger we will start to accept it as the norm, and pattern our own behaviour to comply with external expectations, to the detriment of our free will.

The "datafication" of our lives is an undeniable trend which is impacting all of us. However, its societal consequences are not predetermined. We need to have an open discussion about its nature and implications, and about the kind of society we want to live in.

10 October 2016

⇨ The above information is reprinted with kind permission from *The Conversation*. Please visit www.theconversation.com for further information.

© 2010–2017, The Conversation Trust (UK)

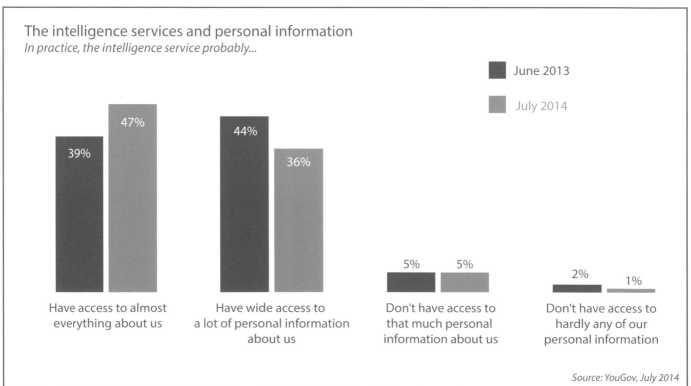

The intelligence services and personal information
In practice, the intelligence service probably...

■ June 2013
■ July 2014

	June 2013	July 2014
Have access to almost everything about us	39%	47%
Have wide access to a lot of personal information about us	44%	36%
Don't have access to that much personal information about us	5%	5%
Don't have access to hardly any of our personal information	2%	1%

Source: YouGov, July 2014

These 48 government organisations can see your Internet history, even if you delete it

By Thomas Tamblyn

I f you think GCHQ are the only ones that can view your browsing history you might want to think again.

The newly enforced Investigatory Powers Bill gives 48 government agencies access to your internet connection records; a log of which internet services you've accessed. These include which websites you've visited and even when you've used instant messaging apps.

Now that the Snoopers' Charter has come into force the Bill is being examined with a fine toothpick to find out just what it means for us and our personal information.

In case you're wondering just what these organisations are then you can send your thanks to Chris Yiu, a blogger who has combed through the Bill and discovered which government agencies will have access to this information.

⇨ Metropolitan Police Service

⇨ City of London Police

⇨ Police forces maintained under section two of the Police Act 1996

⇨ Police Service of Scotland

⇨ Police Service of Northern Ireland

⇨ British Transport Police

⇨ Ministry of Defence Police

⇨ Royal Navy Police

⇨ Royal Military Police

⇨ Royal Air Force Police

⇨ Security Service

⇨ Secret Intelligence Service

⇨ GCHQ

⇨ Ministry of Defence

⇨ Department of Health

⇨ Home Office

⇨ Ministry of Justice

⇨ National Crime Agency

⇨ HM Revenue & Customs

⇨ Department for Transport

⇨ Department for Work & Pensions

⇨ NHS trusts and foundation trusts in England that provide ambulance services

⇨ Common Services Agency for the Scottish Health Service

⇨ Competition and Markets Authority

- ⇨ Criminal Cases Review Commission
- ⇨ Department for Communities in Northern Ireland
- ⇨ Department for the Economy in Northern Ireland
- ⇨ Department of Justice in Northern Ireland
- ⇨ Financial Conduct Authority
- ⇨ Fire and rescue authorities under the Fire and Rescue Services Act 2004
- ⇨ Food Standards Agency
- ⇨ Food Standards Scotland
- ⇨ Gambling Commission
- ⇨ Gangmasters and Labour Abuse Authority
- ⇨ Health and Safety Executive
- ⇨ Independent Police Complaints Commissioner
- ⇨ Information Commissioner
- ⇨ NHS Business Services Authority
- ⇨ Northern Ireland Ambulance Service Health and Social Care Trust
- ⇨ Northern Ireland Fire and Rescue Service Board
- ⇨ Northern Ireland Health and Social Care Regional Business Services Organisation
- ⇨ Office of Communications
- ⇨ Office of the Police Ombudsman for Northern Ireland
- ⇨ Police Investigations and Review Commissioner
- ⇨ Scottish Ambulance Service Board
- ⇨ Scottish Criminal Cases Review Commission
- ⇨ Serious Fraud Office
- ⇨ Welsh Ambulance Services National Health Service Trust

In his blog, titled "Who can view my Internet history", Yiu doesn't mince his words when it comes to expressing how he feels.

"I always wondered what it would feel like to be suffocated by the sort of state intrusion that citizens are subjected to in places like China, Russia and Iran. I guess we're all about to find out."

Boasting some of the most invasive surveillance laws we've ever seen, the Investigatory Powers Bill includes bulk data collection, the forced surveillance of personal devices (in extreme cases) and the ability to even control those devices if possible.

We spoke to John Shaw, VP Product Management at Sophos about how the Bill could affect us and whether we should be worried.

Shaw presented an alternative point of view which is that while the Bill is indeed invasive, it's the indirect actions of the Bill which could pose the most amount of danger to us.

"We should perhaps be more nervous that a hacker might break into the store of data held by your ISP and sell it on." explains Shaw.

"Especially after the revelations about TalkTalk, one of the ISPs that will need to store the data. The Government's advisers claim that there will be very strict controls on the storing and security of the data. But I for one feel nervous about that, and that is the thing that might cause me to use a VPN."

25 November 2016

- ⇨ The above information is reprinted with kind permission from The Huffington Post UK. Please visit www. huffingtonpost.co.uk for further information.

With the latest WikiLeaks revelations about the CIA – is privacy really dead?

In the wake of James Comey's declaration that there's no privacy in America and more WikiLeaks disclosures, do the law and technology prove him right?

By Olivia Solon

In the week that WikiLeaks revealed the CIA and MI5 have an armoury of surveillance tools that can spy on people through their smart TVs, cars and cellphones, the FBI director, James Comey, has said that Americans should not have expectations of "absolute privacy".

"There is no such thing as absolute privacy in America: there is no place outside of judicial reach," Comey said at a Boston College conference on cybersecurity. The remark came as he was discussing the rise of encryption since Edward Snowden's 2013 revelations of the NSA's mass surveillance tools, used on citizens around the world.

Both the Snowden revelations and the CIA leak highlight the variety of creative techniques intelligence agencies can use to spy on individuals, at a time when many of us are voluntarily giving up our personal data to private companies and installing so-called "smart" devices with microphones (smart TVs, Amazon Echo) in our homes.

So, where does this leave us? Is privacy really dead, as Silicon Valley luminaries such as Mark Zuckerberg have previously declared?

Not according to the Electronic Frontier Foundation's executive director, Cindy Cohn.

"The freedom to have a private conversation – free from the worry that a hostile government, a rogue government agent or a competitor or a criminal are listening – is central to a free society," she said.

While not as strict as privacy laws in Europe, the fourth amendment to the US constitution does guarantee the right to be free from unreasonable searches and seizures.

That doesn't mean citizens have 'absolute privacy'.

"I don't think there's been absolute privacy in the history of mankind," said Albert Gidari, director of privacy at the Stanford Center for Internet and Society. "You walk out in public and it's no longer private. You shout from one window to another and someone will hear you in conversation."

"At the same time things are more intrusive, persistent, searchable, they never die. So our conception of what is or isn't risk from a privacy perspective does change and evolve over time."

The law hasn't kept pace with digital technologies. For example, there is a legal theory called the "third-party doctrine" that holds that people who give up their information to third parties like banks, phone companies, social networks and ISPs have "no reasonable expectation of privacy". This has allowed the US Government to obtain information without legal warrants.

Unlike the NSA techniques revealed by Snowden, the CIA appears to favour a more targeted approach: less dragnet, more spearfishing.

The WikiLeaks files show that the CIA has assembled a formidable arsenal of cyberweapons designed to target individuals' devices such as mobile phones, laptops and TVs by targeting the operating systems such as Android, iOS and Windows with malware.

It's encouraging to note that the Government has yet to crack the encryption of secure messaging apps such as WhatsApp, Signal and Confide. However, it does not need to if it can instal malware on people's devices that can collect audio and message traffic before encryption is applied.

Gidari isn't that surprised. "It confirms what everyone saw in last week's episode of *24*. People expect these tools to exist," he said, adding that people were more surprised that the

FBI was initially incapable of breaking into the San Bernardino killer's iPhone.

"People expect the Government to have these magic tools," he said.

American citizens should not be lulled into a false sense of security that the CIA only targets foreign nationals. The 'Vault 7' documents show a broad exchange of tools and information between the CIA, the National Security Agency, and other US federal agencies, as well as intelligence services of close allies Australia, Canada, New Zealand and the United Kingdom.

"We can't spy on our own citizens but we can spy on anyone else's," explained Neil Richards, a law professor from Washington University. "If agencies are friends with each other, they have everybody else do their work for them and they just share the data."

"Dividing the world into American citizens and non-American citizens is a false dichotomy," Gidari added. "We don't have a monopoly on spy tools."

This leaves us with a terrifying new prospect: government spies essentially deploying viruses and trojans against their own citizens.

The onus is now on the companies that make the devices to plug any holes in their operating systems – something they do regularly through bug bounty programs, where security researchers disclose vulnerabilities in return for rewards.

It's clear from the CIA files that the US Government has flouted this custom in order to stockpile "zero days" – undisclosed exploits – for its own advantage. This is a practice the US Government has previously publicly denied.

"If companies aren't aware that a vulnerability exists they can't patch it. If it exists it can be exploited by any malicious actor – whether that's a hacker, foreign state or criminal enterprise," said Neema Singh Guliani, legislative counsel with the American Civil Liberties Union.

"I have a big problem with the Government leaving us vulnerable to the same tools in hand so other nation states and hackers could exploit them," Gidari said. "That isn't protecting American citizens."

Gidari's view echoes Apple's stance when the FBI demanded the company build a backdoor to the iPhone so they could access data on the San Bernardino killer's phone.

"Apple believes deeply that people in the United States and around the world deserve data protection, security and privacy. Sacrificing one for the other only puts people and countries at greater risk," the company said at the time. The iPhone maker was more muted in its response to the Vault 7 dump, vowing to "rapidly address" any security holes.

"There is nearly universal consensus from technologists that it's impossible to build weaknesses or access mechanisms into technology that can only be used by the good guys and not the bad," Cohn said.

This week's revelations are sure to increase the strain on relations between Silicon Valley and the US Government. While some of the older telephony companies such as AT&T and Verizon, which rely heavily on government contracts, have a history of compliance with government requests, tech giants Google, Facebook, Microsoft and Apple have proved to be less compliant.

It's not possible to meaningfully participate in modern life without relationships with some or all of these technology companies processing our data, Richards added. So it's important to know where their loyalties lie – to their customers or to government.

Since Snowden's revelations of mass surveillance, companies such as Apple, Google and Microsoft have been working hard to rebuild trust with consumers through strengthening security, fighting government data requests and releasing transparency reports highlighting when and how many requests are made.

"It's a very encouraging development if we care about civil liberties and the right to privacy, but at the same time it's unsatisfying if the discretion of a company is the only real protection for our data," Richards said.

"We need to build the digital society we want rather than the one handed to us by default," he added.

This will require a complete overhaul of the laws relating to when the Government can collect location and content information, something civil liberty campaigners have been pushing for.

"These decisions need to be made by the public, not by law enforcement or tech executives sitting in private," Richards said.

9 March 2017

⇨ The above information is reprinted with kind permission from *The Guardian*. Please visit www.theguardian.com for further information.

What is mass surveillance?

Mass surveillance is the subjection of a population or significant component of a group to indiscriminate monitoring. It involves a systematic interference with people's right to privacy. Any system that generates and collects data on individuals without attempting to limit the dataset to well-defined targeted individuals is a form of mass surveillance.

Under the methods that mass surveillance is now capable of being conducted, governments can capture virtually all aspects of our lives. Today it increasingly involves the generation, collection and processing of information about large numbers of people, often without any regard to whether they are legally suspected of wrongdoing. At this scale, modern surveillance shifts the burden of proof, leads to an unaccountable increase in power, and has a chilling effect on individual action.

Is mass surveillance only a recent phenomenon?

While the mass surveillance of populations is currently on the rise, mainly due to rapid technological changes around the world, it has been used all throughout history.

One of the oldest forms of mass surveillance are national databases. These old administrative surveillance techniques include censuses registering the subjects of a kingdom, ID documenting individuals and tattoos marking them, and numbering and categorising humans.

The searchable nature of databases makes any datastore a potential investigative tool and increases the potential of trawling. This is why national databases are supposed to be regulated carefully under law in democratic societies.

Census databases collect detailed information on individuals in a country but should not be used to identify specific individuals or populations. Identity schemes should be limited to very specific uses and not allow for discrimination or for abusive use of stop-and-identify powers. The increasing use of biometrics and the ability to query identity databases for matches and near-matches allows for fishing expeditions that increase the risk of abuse and re-use of the system for other purposes than for which it was designed.

Mass surveillance in public spaces became more commonplace with the deployment of closed-circuit television cameras (CCTV). Older systems collected vague images with limited capabilities of linking captured images to personal information. But now it is possible for people's movements to be tracked and stored for later analysis. Automated and real-time identification of large numbers of people is now undertaken, and the risk of further abuses is growing.

What are the latest forms of mass surveillance?

While databases and CCTV still exist and are in use, the most recent discussions around mass surveillance focus around the monitoring of communications, including what we do on our phones and our computers.

When it comes to spying on our phones, government authorities can now get access to data on everyone within a specific geographic area around a cell tower through bulk access to data held by mobile phone companies (often referred to as a 'cell tower dump'). We are also seeing an increase in the use of mobile surveillance tools that allow authorities to monitor all

communications and identify all devices within a localised area, for instance at a public protest by setting up fake mobile base stations.

Having started as mechanisms to administer and control large populations, then moving to capture 'public' actions, mass surveillance techniques are no longer restricted to public-facing activities. For instance, governments have passed laws mandating that all communications transactions are logged and retained by service providers to ensure that they are accessible to government authorities upon request. However, numerous courts have called this type of surveillance policy an interference with the right to privacy.

The technologies of mass surveillance are becoming more prevalent, and as resource limitations disappear, the capabilities for governments become endless. Now it is possible to monitor and retain an entire country's communications content, and directly access communications and metadata from undersea cable companies, telephone companies and Internet service providers.

There are practically no limits on what governments can do with this broad access and the power that comes with unaccountable surveillance. For instance, in conducting fibre optic cable interception states can collect and read any of the content of any unencrypted communication flowing through that cable – including phone calls, voice-over-IP calls, messages, emails, photos and social networking activity. They can then apply a range of analysis techniques and filters to that information – from voice, text and facial recognition, to the mapping of networks and relationships, to behavioural analysis, to emotion detection.

Mass surveillance will be applied beyond communications surveillance. As we move towards 'smart' devices and cities, more and more of our activities will be collected and analysed. Smart meters report on our electricity usage, while smart cities track individuals and vehicles using cameras and sensors. Laws must keep up to date with these innovations that seek to monitor and profile us all. As the UN Office of the High Commissioner for Human Rights noted in 2014, "The technological platforms upon which global political, economic and social life are increasingly reliant are not only vulnerable to mass surveillance, they may actually facilitate it."

What are the legal frameworks around mass surveillance?

Mass surveillance is an indiscriminate measure. Human rights laws require that any interference with privacy is legitimate, necessary in a democratic society and proportionate. Even where it can be shown to meet a legitimate aim, mass surveillance is unlikely to meet the tests of proportionality and necessity.

Key to this is that governments are often reluctant to introduce necessary safeguards to minimise the information that is collected – ID programs are increasingly collecting more information and being required for more transactions; DNA database laws resist the deletion of unnecessary information including the samples and profiles of innocent people; and communications surveillance programs are increasingly trying to 'collect it all'.

In judging whether mass surveillance is lawful, courts have weighed on the scope of the surveillance, the safeguards in place, the type of surveillance and the severity of the pressing social need. They have concluded that the collection and retention of information on people is an act of surveillance that must be controlled. The mere capability to enable surveillance that examines, uses, and stores information consitutes an interference with the right to privacy. The systematic collection, processing and retention of a searchable database of personal information, even of a relatively routine kind, involves a significant interference with the right to respect for private life, and to an emerging extent, requires protection against unreasonable searches.

What's the problem with "collecting everything"?

Governments have been quick to attempt to colour the discourse around mass surveillance by rebranding their actions as "bulk collection" of communications, asserting that such collection in itself is a benign measure that does not offend privacy rights.

But what governments often do not point out is that collection of this information is where the interference to our privacy occurs. Mass surveillance programs are premised on one fundamental objective – collect everything. Mine it, exploit it, extrapolate from it; look for correlations and patterns, suspicious thoughts or words, tenuous relationships or connections.

By starting from a position where everyone is a suspect, mass surveillance encourages the establishment of erroneous correlations and unfair suppositions. It enables individuals to be linked together on the basis of information that

may be no more than a coincidence – a tube ride shared together, a website visited at the same time, a phone connecting to the same cell tower – and conclusions to be drawn about the nature of those links.

Authorities can now have access to information concerning the entirety of an individual's life: everything they do, say, think, send, buy, imbibe, record and obtain, everywhere they go and with whom, from when they wake up in the morning until when they go to sleep. Even the strongest of legal frameworks to govern mass surveillance with the strictest of independent oversight would leave room for abuse of power and misuse of information; for discriminatory attitudes and structural biases; and for human fallibility and malice.

The threat of being subject to such abuse, discrimination or error strikes results in changes in human behaviour, and consequently changes the way we act, speak, and communicate. This is the "chilling effect" of surveillance: the spectre of surveillance may limit, inhibit or dissuade someone's legitimate exercise of his or her rights.

These impacts include not only the violation of privacy rights, but extend to broader societal impacts on the ability to freely form and express ideas and opinions, to associate and organise, and to disagree with dominant political ideologies and demand change to the status quo.

As the UN Special Rapporteur on Freedom of Expression concluded in his 2013 report, states cannot ensure that individuals are able to freely seek and receive information or express themselves without respecting, protecting and promoting their right to privacy. We believe that ultimately mass surveillance will enforce conformity, limit innovation, hamper creation and diminish imagination.

⇨ The above information is reprinted with kind permission from Privacy International. Please visit www.privacyinternational. org for further information.

Human rights and CCTV

The use of CCTV in the UK, and its impact on human rights and civil liberties, regularly hits the headlines. Concerns are raised both about the number of CCTV cameras in the UK and the lack of regulation regarding their use. The UK's Coalition government have said that they intend to introduce a programme of government which sees greater protection for, and a restoration of, civil liberties in the UK. Amongst the areas they have said that they intend to address is an increase in the regulation of CCTV use.

UK – CCTV nation?

Research conducted in 2002 suggested that there were 4.2 million CCTV cameras in the UK – equating to one CCTV camera for every 14 people. So startling was this statistic that it has been seized upon by critics of CCTV ever since. However, this figure was based on an extrapolation from a survey conducted in one area of London and now seems likely to be unreliable.

Comprehensive records of the number of CCTV cameras in the UK are not kept but a 2009 report suggested that the true figure for CCTV cameras in the UK is about 3.2 million. Whilst this represents a significant drop from the earlier estimate, it is widely accepted as proof that the UK has more CCTV cameras than any other country in the world.

Who is using CCTV?

The principal use of CCTV cameras may be by the police and other public authorities to combat crime and antisocial behaviour. However, private businesses – and even individuals – are increasingly turning to CCTV as a means of monitoring and protecting their property. Advances in CCTV technology have resulted in cameras that may have face recognition capabilities, allowing individuals to be picked out of a crowd from a database, or which can monitor for particular types of, suspicious, behaviour.

Are CCTV cameras a deterrent?

Despite the advances in technology some remain sceptical about the efficacy of CCTV in reducing the level of crime. If cameras are everywhere people may become inured to them and they may lose their deterrent effect. In addition, the cameras must be constantly maintained in order for useful data to be produced by them. Firm evidence that the use of CCTV cameras in the UK has had a positive impact on crime figures has not been forthcoming.

Human rights and the use of CCTV

Article 8 of the European Convention on Human Rights concerns the right to family and private life. This includes the right to respect for an individual's home and correspondence. The right contained in Article 8 is known as a qualified right which means that there may be circumstances in which some interference with it is justifiable. This right means that an individual has the right to the level of personal privacy which is compatible with a democratic society, taking into account the equivalent rights and freedoms of others. Any interference with this right by a public authority may be subject to a test of acceptability.

The state and public authorities are permitted to interfere with an individual's Article 8 right to privacy if the interference has an obvious legal justification. Amongst other reasons, this could be because the interference is necessary to protect national security or for the prevention of crime. In addition to having a clear legal justification, the amount of interference with the right must be proportionate to the end result achieved and only go as far as is required to achieve that result.

Public authorities, including the police and local councils, must balance the benefits of using CCTV against an individual's right to privacy.

CCTV and data protection

The problem for an individual's personal privacy is that if a camera is installed by a private company or an individual to monitor their own property there is little legal protection for any individual being observed by it. Nonetheless, there may be issues regarding the use and storage of any images captured by the CCTV camera.

The Data Protection Act 1998 governs the use of CCTV equipment and any data produced or stored by it. The Act is likely to apply if a CCTV camera is set up, in public place, to capture everything that passes in front of it. The owner of the CCTV equipment will have to comply with any relevant provisions of the Act. However, a householder who sets up a CCTV camera for purely 'domestic purposes' may not have to comply with the Data Protection Act. The only recourse for an individual who feels they are being unreasonably targeted by such a CCTV camera – for example, one belonging to an unfriendly neighbour – could be to make a complaint to the police about harassment.

1 March 2017

⇨ The above information is reprinted with kind permission from About Human Rights. Please visit www.abouthumanrights.co.uk for further information.

© About Human Rights 2017

Surveillance and counter-terrorism

How to make applications under the Regulation of Investigatory Powers Act (RIPA) and how the Government responds to terrorist incidents.

Overview

This guide provides information on how the Government regulates surveillance and what the Government does in the event of a terrorist incident.

It includes details on how to make an application under the Regulation of Investigatory Powers Act 2000 (RIPA) and explains when RIPA applies and what RIPA does.

It also covers the Government's counter-terrorism plans, including central and local crisis response, how the Government communicates with the public and advice on staying safe during terrorism threats.

RIPA: what it is and how to apply

RIPA is the law governing the use of covert techniques by public authorities. It requires that when public authorities, such as the police or government departments, need to use covert techniques to obtain private information about someone, they do it in a way that is necessary, proportionate, and compatible with human rights.

RIPA's guidelines and codes apply to actions such as:

⇨ intercepting communications, such as the content of telephone calls, emails or letters

⇨ acquiring communications data: the 'who, when and where' of communications, such as a telephone billing or subscriber details

⇨ conducting covert surveillance, either in private premises or vehicles (intrusive surveillance) or in public places (directed surveillance)

⇨ the use of covert human intelligence sources, such as informants or undercover officers

⇨ access to electronic data protected by encryption or passwords.

RIPA applies to a wide range of investigations in which private information might be obtained. Cases in which it applies include:

⇨ terrorism

⇨ crime

⇨ public safety

⇨ emergency services.

To make an application under RIPA on behalf of a public authority, download the appropriate codes of practice and application forms.

All the codes on this website can also be purchased from The Stationery Office.

Local authority use of RIPA

Local authorities have a wide range of functions and are responsible in law for enforcing over 100 separate Acts of Parliament. In particular, local authorities investigate offences in the following areas:

⇨ trading standards, including action taken against loan sharks and rogue traders, consumer scams, sale of counterfeit goods, unsafe toys and electrical goods

⇨ environmental health, including action against large-scale waste dumping, dangerous workplaces, pest control and the sale of unfit food

⇨ benefit fraud, including action to counter fraudulent claims for housing benefits, investigating 'living together' and 'working whilst in receipt of benefit' allegations and council tax evasion.

Local authorities are also responsible for tackling issues as diverse as anti-social behaviour, unlicensed gambling, threats to children in care, underage employment and taxi regulation. As part of their investigation a local authority may consider that it is appropriate to use a RIPA technique to obtain evidence.

Local authorities use three investigatory techniques that can be authorised under RIPA:

⇨ directed surveillance

⇨ use of a covert human intelligence source

⇨ obtaining and disclosing communications data.

RIPA does not allow the use of any other covert techniques by local authorities to be authorised. In particular, a local authority cannot be authorised under RIPA to intercept the content of a communication.

Approval of local authority use of RIPA

From 1 November 2012, local authorities are required to obtain judicial approval prior to using covert techniques. Local authority authorisations and notices under RIPA will only be given effect once an order has been granted by a justice of the peace in England and Wales, a sheriff in Scotland and a district judge (magistrates' court) in Northern Ireland.

Additionally, from this date local authority use of directed surveillance under RIPA will be limited to the investigation of crimes which attract a six month or more custodial sentence, with the exception of offences relating to the underage sale of alcohol and tobacco.

Responding to a terrorist incident

In a terrorist attack, the Home Secretary leads the government response to the incident as the minister responsible for counter-terrorism in England, Wales and Scotland.

Effective command and control is essential to successfully manage a counter-terrorist incident. The UK's approach to emergency response and recovery is founded on an approach in which operations and decisions are made at the lowest appropriate level.

⇨ The above information is reprinted with kind permission from GOV. UK. Please visit GOV.UK for further information.

© Crown copyright 2017

Broad support for increased surveillance powers

British people say the police and intelligence agencies should retain all of their communications data for 12 months – but tend to oppose a ban on encryption software.

The attack on French satirical magazine *Charlie Hebdo* last week has added fresh impetus to the Conservatives' ongoing struggle to introduce new surveillance legislation. The Draft Communications Data Bill 2012 (dubbed the 'snoopers charter') would have extended data retention obligations on communications companies to include the metadata of social media, email and Internet voice calls; however, it was blocked by the Lib Dems. Now there is even greater need for such legislation, says David Cameron, because newer forms of encrypted communication such as WhatsApp and Snapchat may be 'unreadable' by intelligence.

YouGov research for the *Sunday Times* finds the British public supportive of increasing the security services' access to public communications in order to fight terrorism (by 52–31%).

Most people (53%) say that, specifically, phone and Internet companies should be required to retain everyone's internet browsing history, emails, voice calls, social media interactions and mobile messaging, which the police and intelligence agencies would be able to access for anti-terrorism purposes. 31% would oppose giving the security forces these powers.

The 2012 Communications Data Bill required security services to receive a warrant from the Home Secretary before they could access the content – not merely the who,

when, where and how (the metadata) – of a communication. By 51–35% the public support this qualification, as

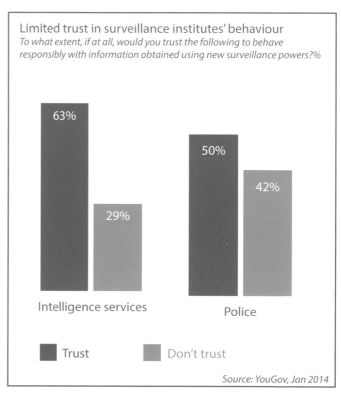

Limited trust in surveillance institutes' behaviour
To what extent, if at all, would you trust the following to behave responsibly with information obtained using new surveillance powers?%

Intelligence services: Trust 63%, Don't trust 29%
Police: Trust 50%, Don't trust 42%

■ Trust   ■ Don't trust

Source: YouGov, Jan 2014

opposed to giving intelligence agencies their own general powers of access.

Doubts certainly exist over the trustworthiness of institutions who could be granted the new powers however. While there is a tendency to trust MI5 and MI6 to behave responsibly (63% trust, 29% do not), there is near division over the trustworthiness of the police to do so (50% trust, 42% do not), and clear uncertainty with regards to politicians and civil servants (45% trust, 46% do not).

And despite the general willingness to offer up personal data in the fight for security, there does seem to be a red line: 43% would oppose a ban on encryption software, while 29% would support it.

The special relationship

David Cameron has been in Washington this week, meeting with Barack Obama to discuss bolstering the US and UK economies, on Thursday, and getting technology companies like Facebook and Google to permit government access to encrypted messages, on Friday.

British media has been positive about the visit, taking it as a sign of the 'special relationship' that exists between the two countries. British people themselves, however, while agreeing the relationship is close (61%), say the relationship is not in fact special – "it's just like those with other British allies", say 52%.

18 January 2015

⇨ The above information is reprinted with kind permission from YouGov. Please visit www.yougov.co.uk for further information.

Army's 'watchkeeper' drone to fly above british skies

A huge unmanned drone is set to fly above UK skies this week ahead of trials in Afghanistan.

Watchkeeper, a reconnaissance and surveillance unmanned air system (UAS), has a wingspan of 35 feet and can fly at an altitude of up to 16,000 feet.

It has been designed to loiter over areas of interest for "significantly longer" than existing systems, providing clear surveillance pictures to troops on the ground.

Above: The aircraft boasts two sensors – a day and night camera which produces 24-hour high-definition images and a radar sensor, allowing it to see in all conditions.

The images it produces are relayed in real time to a ground control station that acts as the aircraft's cockpit – reducing the need to deploy troops to "potentially dangerous" situations.

Watchkeeper, which has been tested in West Wales since 2010 and is nearing the end of its trials, is expected to take a "significant role" in future military campaigns.

This week, highly-skilled pilots will fly Watchkeeper in restricted airspace over the Ministry of Defence's Salisbury Plain Training Area in Wiltshire, overseen by military air traffic controllers.

The Army is due to begin its own training later this year.

Colonel Mark Thornhill, Commander of 1st Artillery Brigade said: "Watchkeeper is a state-of-the-art system coming in to service now. It can fly for longer, it flies off rough strips, it has better sensors.

"Watchkeeper is designed specifically to support worldwide operations in many different locations.

"Watchkeeper is a fantastic capability because it will allow us to provide real-time imagery back to the ground commander so that he can then take appropriate action depending on what he sees and what he learns from that imagery.

"Therefore, he will be able to perform in a much better fashion and make much better operational decisions based on the imagery we are providing to him."

Watchkeeper, which is being developed by Thales UK, is unarmed and does not carry any weapons. It has already clocked up 500 hours of flying time in West Wales.

The Army currently operates four types of UAS in Afghanistan, which play an important role protecting soldiers on the ground by providing them with intelligence and reducing the need for deployment. Watchkeeper will provide additional capability to the fleet - which has already completed 120,000 flying hours - once in service this summer.

Lance Corporal Christopher Gazey, a UAS analyst for 1st Artillery Brigade, said images produced by Watchkeeper would help give the Army better situational awareness.

"You can tell the difference between a man, a woman and a child, but obviously you are not going to do the Hollywood stuff of seeing what people are typing on their phones," Lance Corporal Gazey said.

24 February 2014

⇨ The above information is reprinted with kind permission from *The Huffington Post UK*. Please visit www.huffingtonpost.co.uk for further information.

Sweden: national DNA database could soon be released to law enforcement and private companies

Sweden has been collecting newborn DNA samples since 1975.

By India Ashok

So far jealously guarded, research-only national DNA database in Sweden may soon be made available to law enforcement and private firms, including insurance companies. The Swedish Government began collecting blood samples of newborn babies in 1975, with the approval of parents, in efforts to aid medical research into phenylketonuria (PKU) – a genetic metabolic deficiency.

The DNA database, in time, has become one of the world's most comprehensive registries, which contains genetic information on every Swedish citizen under the age of 43, *Ars Technica* reported. The database so far has been off limits, except to the medical research community. There have been very rare instances of the police being allowed to have access to the database, especially after a law was implemented which required the police to obtain a court order to gain access to the database.

The Swedish Government recently commissioned an inquiry aimed at determining the management and use of the DNA database, which has been maintained by the Karolinska University Hospital. It will look into the possibility of making the registry available not only to law enforcement agencies but also to private firms. Rick Falkvinge, the founder of the Pirate Party in Sweden, declared the move to be "an outrageous and audacious breach of contract".

Falkvinge added: "The instant there's a mere suspicion that this will be used against the sampled newborn in the future – as is the case now – instead of being used for the good of humanity as a whole, people won't provide the DNA database with more samples, or at least not enough samples to provide researchable coverage."

The database was originally created for purely medical research purposes and is considered to be an invaluable trove for the scientific research community. However, researchers and privacy activists have expressed concerns about the possible repercussions and privacy infringement, in the event of the DNA database being made available to law enforcement and private firms.

Falkvinge told IBTimes UK: "It's also noteworthy that the PKU register isn't useful for Hollywood-movie-style police 'fishing expeditions', as it's really just one blood sample per individual. It's not sequenced and sampled and searchable against a random sample. What it is, though, is that if already you know the specific individual you want to match against, you would be able to find their blood sample in this register and compare against that one specifically."

He added: "Legislators tend to forget that law enforcement isn't the single most important task in society. Law enforcement exists for a purpose – to uphold our liberty, our values, our community. When law enforcement is given powers that destroy those values and that purpose, it becomes counterproductive and more dangerous than the crime it's fighting."

17 July 2017

⇨ The above information is reprinted with kind permission from the *International Business Times*. Please visit www.ibtimes.co.uk for further information.

Drones

The ICO recommends that users of drones – also called unmanned aerial systems (UAS) or unmanned aerial vehicles (UAVs) – with cameras should operate them in a responsible way to respect the privacy of others.

Are drones covered by the Data Protection Act (DPA)?

If a drone has a camera, its use has the potential to be covered by the DPA.

Is it OK to use drones with cameras?

If you are using a drone with a camera, there could be a privacy risk to other people. Follow our tips below to help ensure you respect people's privacy when using your drone.

How can I use my drone responsibly?

Tips on responsible use of drones:

⇨ Let people know before you start recording. In some scenarios this is going to be quite easy because you will know everyone within close view (for example, if you are taking a group photo at a family barbeque). In other scenarios, for example at the beach or the park, this is going to be much more difficult so you'll need to apply some common sense before you start.

⇨ Consider your surroundings. If you are recording images beyond your home, a drone may intrude on the privacy of others where they expect their privacy to be respected (such as in their back garden). It is unlikely that you would want a drone to be hovering outside your window so be considerate to others and don't hover outside theirs.

⇨ Get to know your camera first. It is a good idea to get to know the capability of your camera in a controlled situation to understand how it works. What is the quality of the image? How powerful is the zoom? Can you control when it starts and stops recording? Drone cameras are capable of taking unusual and creative pictures from original vantage points. Knowing the capabilities of your camera will help you to reduce the risk of privacy intrusion.

⇨ Plan your flight. Your drone's battery life is likely to be short. By understanding its capabilities you will be able to make best use of its flight and it will be easier to plan how to avoid invading the privacy of other people. For example, it may be more privacy-friendly to launch from a different location rather than flying close to other people or their property.

⇨ Keep you and your drone in view. You won't want to lose it, and if you are clearly visible then it will be easier for members of the public to know that you are the person responsible for the drone.

⇨ Think before sharing. Once your drone has landed, think carefully about who's going to be looking at the images, particularly if you're thinking about posting them on social media. Avoid sharing images that could have unfair or harmful consequences. Apply the same commonsense approach that you would with images or video recorded by a smartphone or digital camera.

⇨ Keep the images safe. The images you have taken may be saved on an SD card or USB drive attached to the drone or the camera. If they are not necessary, then don't keep them. If you do want to keep them, then make sure they are kept in a safe place.

Other laws

⇨ Other laws that protect individuals from harassment may apply when using your drone. It is worth checking which laws you need to be aware of before you fly your drone to avoid any unexpected complaints or disputes.

⇨ The safe use of drones is regulated by the Civil Aviation Authority. For guidance about this, see UAS on the Civil Aviation Authority website.

Can I use my drone for work?

As with personal use, if you are using your drone for a more formal, professional purpose, then it is important that you understand your legal obligations as a data controller as the situation will be different.

For more information, read the CCTV code (for organisations), which has a section about drones (referred to as UAS in the code).

⇨ The above information is reprinted with kind permission from the Information Commissioner's Office. Please visit www.ico.org.uk for further information.

© Information Commissioner's Office 2017

The 'Internet of Things' – what is it and what are the legal issues?

By Mairead Powell

The 'Internet of Things' (IoT) is a term used to describe devices which can connect via the Internet and can communicate with us and each other. Used efficiently, these IoT devices could transform the way in which we live, with technology assisting various tasks and processes as we go about our daily lives.

There is a whole host of IoT devices now available to consumers which promise to make life smarter, from smart TVs to smart cars to smart pet feeders.

As an example, my friend recently had a new boiler fitted, along with a shiny little box which cleverly self-programmes to her temperature needs. This little box knows when she is at home or away, awake or asleep and through a connection with her phone she can turn the heating on whilst out of the house. It is evident that such technology could bring huge benefits, including cost and time savings, but what are the legal issues that should be considered?

The legal issues

Data, data and more data – security risk?

Data security is a key concern with IoT devices, taking into account just how much data can be collected. With various IoT devices talking to each other via the internet, the potential for a data security breach is high and with more and more IoT devices coming onto the market, this issue is not going to go away.

Take for example the smart meter initiative led by the Government. The intention is that by 2020, over 53 million smart meters shall be installed in over 30 million homes and small businesses. The potential here for households and small businesses to join the 'grid' and be connected through an IoT device is huge.

With increased data collection, comes an increase in the risk of a breach or failure in data security. As previously mentioned, my friend's shiny new box knows when she is at home or away. Is there a risk that this information could end up in the wrong hands? Absolutely, and to make matters worse, some IoT devices have not been designed to automatically update with new security updates and patches, leaving these devices without any security updates. There is also the risk that users may not update default passwords provided with the IoT devices or fail to update them with sufficiently strong passwords.

If hackers infiltrate IoT devices, the potential scope for damage is great. Take for example a smart car – a successful hack could impact the functions and safety of the car. Beyond personal use, IoT devices can be used in various businesses and institutions including hospitals. In hospitals, IoT devices can be used to track the vital information of patients, which medics can use to determine required medication. If these systems were hacked the result could potentially be life threatening. Whilst these examples are extreme, they do highlight the importance of getting security right and ensuring user confidence and trust.

Data protection:

The security of data goes hand in hand with data protection. The current data protection regime in the UK is governed by the Data Protection Act 1998 which controls how personal data is used by

organisations. There have been recent developments in respect of EU data protection law and the new General Data Protection Regulation (GDPR) will come into force on 25 May 2018. Regardless of the UK's EU membership status, any company which holds or uses personal data of EU citizens will still be required to comply with the GDPR. In addition, there is also the likelihood that in preparation to leave the EU, the UK will reform its current data protection law to bring it in line with the GDPR.

With the tightening up of the data protection regime, this will impact on the obligations and responsibilities imposed on those businesses involved in the collection and processing of data from IoT devices – including a requirement to carry out privacy impact assessments, increased scrutiny as to obtaining the consent of the user to process their personal information and enhanced data subject rights, to name but a few.

Adopting a privacy by design approach and incorporating privacy impact assessments into the design stage of the IoT devices should put data privacy at the forefront of the minds of the designers and manufacturers of IoT devices.

Data sovereignty

Linked with data protection is data sovereignty – the principle whereby digital data stored in a country will be subject to the laws of that country. The data from IoT devices may be held in the "cloud" or in a data centre and it is vital to understand where that data resides. For example, if this is in the US, that data would also be subject to the laws of the US. This is particularly relevant given the developments in respect of the Safe Harbour Agreement and the EU-US Privacy Shield. IoT device providers will need to be clued up on where the data is to be located so it is clear which laws and regulations will apply in respect of that data.

Product liability

With the potential for IoT devices to transform the way in which we conduct our daily lives, we have to question what happens in the event these devices get it wrong? Where does the liability sit?

Take for example smart, driverless cars. The potential is for these vehicles to radicalise the way in which we get from A to B. However, what happens in the event the car, whilst in driverless mode, is caught speeding or worst still, what happens if the car causes an accident? Who takes responsibility for this?

Recently, there has been a situation where autopilot driverless technology resulted in the death of the driver – the first known fatality resulting from such technology. That particular car manufacturer has stated that the computer program used in the car is still in a "beta testing phase", this is something which the driver is required to acknowledge prior to using the technology, and that drivers are warned to keep their hands on the wheel at all times and be "prepared to take over at any time". Other car manufacturers have taken the stance that they will take full responsibility for their driverless technology – giving the driver certainty as to how liability would be allocated in the event of an accident. This approach sees a shift on responsibility from the driver to the car manufacturer. However, this approach is not currently the norm.

In support of the progression of driverless technology, the Department for Transport has initiated a consultation in respect of proposed changes to the laws and rules surrounding driverless cars and insurance cover for such technology. Under the proposed new measures, the rules would change, allowing for driverless cars to be insured and the Highway Code and associated regulations will be updated to support the use of driverless car features. No doubt steps such as this will pave the way for new regulations and provide drivers with the added confidence needed when deciding whether to purchase and use such technology.

The future of the 'Internet of Things'

With much investment in the industry, the IoT's market will no doubt continue to grow. Some of the gimmicks may fall by the way side but there is considered to be real benefit to a number of the smart products available today and envisaged for the future.

However, key to the success of the IoT is consumer confidence. Manufacturers will need to convince consumers that the use of IoT devices is safe and secure and to do this, much work is still needed.

30 August 2016

⇨ The above information is reprinted with kind permission from Wright Hassall. Please visit www. wrighthassall.co.uk for further information.

Privacy regulators' study finds 'Internet of Things' shortfalls

Six in ten 'Internet of Things' devices don't properly tell customers how their personal information is being used, an international study has found.

The study, by 25 data protection regulators around the world, looked at devices like smart electricity meters, Internet-connected thermostats and watches that monitor health, considering how well companies communicate privacy matters to their customers.

The report showed:

⇨ 59 per cent of devices failed to adequately explain to customers how their personal information was collected, used and disclosed;

⇨ 68 per cent failed to properly explain how information was stored;

⇨ 72 per cent failed to explain how customers could delete their information off the device and

⇨ 38 per cent failed to include easily identifiable contact details if customers had privacy concerns.

Concerns were also raised around medical devices that sent reports back to GPs via unencrypted email.

The data protection authorities looked at more than 300 devices. Authorities will now consider action against any devices or services thought to have been breaking data protection laws.

The work was coordinated by the Global Privacy Enforcement Network, and follows previous reports on online services for children, website privacy policies and mobile phone apps.

The action is being led by the Information Commissioner's Office (ICO) in the UK. Steve Eckersley, ICO Head of Enforcement, said:

"This technology can improve our homes, our health and our happiness. But that shouldn't be at the cost of our privacy. Companies making these devices need to be clear how they're protecting customers. We would encourage companies to properly consider the privacy impact on individuals before they go to market with their product and services. If consumers are nervous that devices aren't using their data safely and sensibly, then they won't use them.

"By looking at this internationally, we've been able to get an excellent overview on this topic. We'll now be building on that, working with the industry and looking specifically at companies who might not have done enough to comply with the law."

22 September 2016

⇨ The above information is reprinted with kind permission from the Information Commissioner's Office. Please visit www.ico.org.uk for further information.

Why your smart TV is the perfect way to spy on you

By Cara McGoogan

In a world of Internet-connected devices that could be targeted by hackers in a number of ways, it has become common parlance to hear of smartphones and computers being hacked and turned into spying tools. But recently another common device has been added to the roster of possible monitors: smart TVs.

First came the news that Vizio had been tracking customers through their TVs. Then WikiLeaks' latest raft of documents alleged the CIA had created tools to turn smart TVs into bugging devices.

While the news shouldn't come as a surprise, given the endless warnings that our Internet-connected devices can easily be hacked or used to watch us, it adds another piece of technology for us to worry about when thinking of our privacy.

TVs like mobile phones often betray our most intimate lives, often being located in the centre of our homes. They are often fitted with cameras and microphones, as well as internal memories, which can be used to monitor what we're doing, saying and watching.

As a newer Internet-connected device, smart TVs are less likely to receive proper security support. This is in part because users don't expect them, because of the variety of different operating systems, and as security isn't traditionally the remit of TV manufacturers. Added to this, users are less likely to use best security practices when it comes to their TV, such as changing passwords and regularly updating the software.

What is a smart TV?

Smart TVs can connect to the internet to access a range of services such as video streaming, games and apps. They are distinct from traditional TVs which require a set-top box to access on-demand programming and additional functions.

Who could be spying on you through your TV?

Recent news has shown that everyone from manufacturers to advertisers to the intelligence services could be watching you through your TV.

Fears that smart TVs could be watching their owners first arose back in 2015 when one of Samsung's privacy policies warned that all voice recognition data would be passed to a third party. "Be aware that if your spoken words include personal or other sensitive information, that information will be among the data captured and transmitted to a third party through your voice recognition," it said.

Then, earlier this year Vizio was fined $2.2 million (£1.8 million) for tracking users' viewing habits without them knowing and sharing the information.

As well as the manufacturers monitoring viewers, it has now been revealed that intelligence agencies and law enforcement could be watching citizens

---

Tips to secure your iPhone from hackers

1. Use a PIN or fingerprint security

Locking your screen will protect your sensitive data and apps from meddling.

2) Use a longer passphrase

Go to your settings app, then 'Touch ID & Passcode' and turn 'Simple Passcode' off. This will allow you to create a longer and more complex passcode with upper and lowercase letters, numbers and other symbols.

3) Activate self-destruct

You can tell your phone to delete all data if it thinks someone is trying to break in. Under the same page on Settings you can enable 'erase data' – this will wipe the phone clean after ten incorrect guesses at the PIN.

4) Increase your privacy settings

Go into your settings app and then the 'privacy' tab. Here you will be able to see which apps have which privileges, and turn them off/on.

5) Turn off notifications

The ability to see a summary of notifications on the lock screen is handy, but if that gives away personal or confidential data then you could be in trouble. Remember, it will show the contents of messages you receive, your calendar for that day and various other things.

6) Disable Siri

Siri can leak data even when your phone is locked. Go to settings, then 'Touch ID & passcode' and set 'Allow access when locked' on Siri to Off.

7) Type it for yourself

AutoFill is a handy feature that does exactly what it says on the tin: any time that Safari sees a box asking for your name, username, password or credit card details, it fills them in for you. This is fine, unless someone else happens to be using your phone. To turn it off, go to settings, then general and 'Passwords & AutoFill'.

through their TVs. Information released by WikiLeaks claims that MI5 and the CIA had created a "fake off" mode for the Samsung F8000 range that allowed them to secretly record users' conversations through the camera and microphone.

How can you stop them?

TV manufacturers can only monitor customers if they have provided their consent. This is often asked for in the set-up process, but can generally be revoked at a later date in Settings.

Another way to protect yourself is to make sure your TV is running the latest software. You can do this by turning on automatic updates or regularly checking for them in Settings.

Samsung has said it is "urgently" looking into the news that the CIA could have monitored its customers' conversations through the Weeping Angel hack, but has not commented on the validity of the claims. If it finds a problem the company is likely to issue a security update to fix the bug.

8 March 2017

⇨ The above information is reprinted with kind permission from *The Telegraph*. Please visit www.telegraph.co.uk for further information.

Online and out there: how children view privacy differently from adults

An article from The Conversation. THE CONVERSATION

By Joanne Orlando, Senior lecturer, Educational Technology, Western Sydney University

Have you seen the how-to video of a teenage girl styling her hair that went disastrously wrong? She was obviously very disturbed by what happened, yet still uploaded the footage onto YouTube. Do you think a 45- or 50-year-old would upload an equivalent video of themselves?

The majority of young people now share lots of things online that many adults question and feel uncomfortable about: their likes, dislikes, personal views, who they're in a relationship with, where they are, images of themselves and others doing things they should or maybe shouldn't be doing.

In fact, a study undertaken in the US by Pew Research found that 91% of 12- to 17-year-olds posted selfies online, 24% posted videos of themselves. Another 91% were happy posting their real name, 82% their birthday, 71% where they live and the school they attend, 53% their email address and 20% their mobile phone number.

Overstepping

Children's fondness for online sharing is a global phenomenon, and in response governments internationally have initiated awareness campaigns that aim to ensure children are more private online.

In the UK, the National Society for the Prevention of Cruelty to Children recently launched a Share Aware campaign. This includes the recent TV advertisement, called I saw your willy, which depicts the ill-fated consequences of a young boy who, as a joke, texts a photo of his penis to his friend.

The ad emphasises to children the need to keep personal information about themselves offline and private.

Similarly, the Australian Federal Police have launched Cyber safety and ThinkUKnow presentations for school students, which highlights the social problems that can arise when you're having fun online.

Adults often interpret children's constant online sharing to mean that they don't care about privacy and/or don't understand the potential longer-term issues. There is some truth to this perspective. But simply labeling children as either disobedient or naïve is too simplistic. There is an important need to understand why children are overstepping adult-defined marks of privacy online.

Shifting attitudes

In the words of Facebook, our relationship status with privacy can be summed up as: it's complicated.

Part of the complexity comes down to how privacy is defined. Many adults understand privacy to mean being selective about what one reveals about themselves so as not to reveal too much personal information. We often assume that children will adopt the same conceptualisation, but should we?

Privacy is a fluid notion. Think of Victorian times and the imperative for women to keep their ankles hidden. Part of the reason its definition is shaped and reshaped is due to the changing social environment in which we live. This idea is useful for thinking about why children divulge so much information online.

Children are growing up in public (not private) times, in which people freely and constantly reveal themselves on their screens. This is not solely associated with physical nudity and the stream of semi-clad women that constantly inhabit advertisements,

music videos and the like. An environment that idolises nudity certainly contributes to children seeing such behaviour as the norm. Privacy, however, is not just about nudity and sex.

Given the exponential growth of reality shows and social media, children now have unprecedented access to the inner thoughts and personal actions of others. Children are growing up watching real people freely share their deep personal ideas, experiences, opinions and actions. The very purpose of these mediums is to encourage such sharing of information!

Children watch everyday people in the Big Brother house openly discuss their sexual experiences, develop friendships, go to the toilet, get ready after their morning shower, and explain deep personal childhood issues.

Similarly, they watch *Survivor* and *The Bachelor* where people can reveal the darker side of their ambitions, worldviews and ways of dealing with others. Their revelations are under the guise of competition; however, they offer subliminal messages about what we can and should share publicly.

Consistently watching others reveal themselves on screen feeds children's understanding of what is private information and what isn't. Its impact is strengthened because children watch these revelations on their personal screen such as their tablet or mobile, which can make it more of an intimate, one-to-one connection for the child.

Generation gap

Add to this, the dynamic stage in life young people are at, which is characterised by risk-taking behaviour. This combination results in the understanding that sharing what many adults might consider to be private ideas, is really just part of life.

In previous generations it was assumed that the average person wouldn't want to give up privacy. But for this generation, giving up privacy for a social life, fame (or infamy for some), easy access to shopping and studying or working from home is the norm.

Children's penchant for online sharing is a much larger cultural transformation than it's given credit for. The whole idea of what is private and what is public is being disrupted and reshaped by new screen-driven interests and activities.

There is a need to move away from simply judging and reprimanding for their online sharing habits. There is always a need for safety and awareness campaigns, although it is also important to move beyond older and outmoded views of privacy so that we can actually understand young people's privacy negotiations.

In this way we might have more of a chance to meaningfully support negotiations that are transparent, equitable and foster children's well-being.

14 April 2015

⇨ The above information is reprinted with kind permission from *The Conversation*. Please visit www.theconversation.com for further information.

Hackers can hijack WiFi Hello Barbie to spy on your children

Security researcher warns hackers could steal personal information and turn the microphone of the doll into a surveillance device.

By Samuel Gibbs

Mattel's latest WiFi-enabled Barbie doll can easily be hacked to turn it into a surveillance device for spying on children and listening into conversations without the owner's knowledge.

The Hello Barbie doll is billed as the world's first "interactive doll" capable of listening to a child and responding via voice, in a similar way to Apple's Siri, Google's Now and Microsoft's Cortana.

It's just a matter of time until we are able to have her say anything we want

Matt Jakubowski

It connects to the Internet via WiFi and has a microphone to record children and send that information off to third-parties for processing before responding with natural language responses.

But US security researcher Matt Jakubowski discovered that when connected to Wi-Fi the doll was vulnerable to hacking, allowing him easy access to the doll's system information, account information, stored audio files and direct access to the microphone.

Jakubowski told NBC: "You can take that information and find out a person's house or business. It's just a matter of time until we are able to replace their servers with ours and have her say anything we want."

Once Jakubowski took control of where the data was sent the snooping possibilities were apparent. The doll only listens in on a conversation when a button is pressed and the recorded audio is encrypted before being sent over the Internet, but once a hacker has control of the doll the privacy features could be overridden.

It was the ease with which the doll was compromise, that was most concerning. The information stored by the doll could allow hackers to take over a home WiFi network and from there gain access to other internet connected devices, steal personal information and cause other problems for the owners, potentially without their knowledge.

This isn't the first time that Hello Barbie has been placed under the privacy spotlight. On its release in March privacy campaigners warned that a child's intimate conversations with their doll were being recorded and analysed and that it should not go on sale.

With a Hello Barbie in the hands of a child and carried everywhere they and their parents go, it could be the ultimate in audio surveillance device for miscreant hackers.

ToyTalk's chief executive Oren Jacob said: "An enthusiastic researcher has reported finding some device data and called that a hack. While the path that researcher used to find that data is not obvious and not user-friendly, it is important to note that all that information was already directly available to Hello Barbie customers through the Hello Barbie Companion App. No user data, no Barbie content, and no major security nor privacy protections has been compromised to our knowledge."

Mattel, the manufacturers of Hello Barbie, did not respond to requests for comment.

26 November 2015

⇨ The above information is reprinted with kind permission from *The Guardian*. Please visit www.theguardian.com for further information.

Austrian teenager sues parents for sharing childhood photographs on Facebook

A teenager has sued her parents for posting "embarrassing and intimate" baby photos of her on Facebook.

By Sophie Gallagher

The 18-year-old, who lives in Austria, is taking her parents to court as she claims they knew "no shame and no limit" in sharing over 500 photographs of her with their friends online.

Her lawyer Michael Rami, told *The Local* Austria newspaper, that since 2009 her parents have "made her life a misery" by posting pictures of her having her nappy changed and being potty trained.

Michael Rami quotes the claimant saying: "They knew no shame and no limit – and didn't care whether it was a picture of me sitting on the toilet or lying naked in my cot – every stage was photographed and then made public."

The woman has repeatedly asked for the images to be deleted but her parents have refused. She explained: "I'm tired of not being taken seriously by my parents."

The woman's father claims that he has copyright on the images, and a right to distribute them, because he took them.

This case, which will be heard in November, is the first of its kind in Austria.

Rami says his client's case rests on proving that her parents violated her right to a personal life and if she is successful, her parents may have to pay compensation and legal costs.

Austria isn't the only country dealing with the consequences of social media over sharing, in March 2016 new laws were introduced in France to deal with similar situations.

Anyone convicted of publishing images of another person without their consent can face up to a year in prison and a fine of €45,000.

15 September 2016

⇨ The above information is reprinted with kind permission from The Huffington Post UK. Please visit www. huffingtonpost.co.uk for further information.

Sharing pictures of your children online

Most parents love sharing photos of their children with friends and family. But remember – pictures you share online could be out there for ever. Learn how to protect your child whilst staying social.

Are you a 'sharent'?

For many children online life begins before birth, when their excited parents-to-be post ultrasound images on social media. According to a recent poll, the average parent will share their child's image online nearly 1,000 times before their fifth birthday (The Parent Zone, 2015). For parent bloggers the total is likely to be double that, or more.

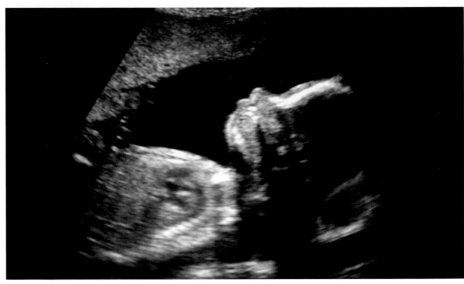

The Internet can provide fantastic tools for sharing special moments from your child's early years with family and friends. And online parenting forums, networks and blogs often provide valuable support and reassurance through parenting's ups and downs.

But before you share, you should give thought to exactly who can see photos and comments featuring your child, and how this online footprint might affect your child in years to come.

What should you consider?

⇨ Who's looking? When did you last check your privacy settings? On most social networks the default is that any other service user can access your pictures, which may also appear in Internet search results. Remember that anyone who can see a photo can also download or screenshot it, and could go on to share it.

⇨ What else are you sharing? You might be sharing more than what's in the post. As default, many cameras, phones and apps tag posts and photos with 'meta-data' which can include location details and other identifying information. This is potentially risky for any child, but poses particular risks for vulnerable children such as those who have been fostered or adopted and could be sought online by members of their birth family.

⇨ Ownership. Under the terms and conditions of most social networks, when you share a photo you license the network to use and reproduce your image, and grant it the right to license it for use by third parties. It could be used for commercial purposes, a point deliberately highlighted by the Danish company Koppie Koppie, which sold mugs featuring freely downloaded pictures of young children. Another online activity which has distressed parents and carers is the 'Baby Role Play' game played by some Instagram users, who repost photographs of other people's children and create fictional identities based on them.

⇨ Their digital tattoo. Every publicly accessible image or comment featuring your child contributes to a public image which will follow them into the future. That apocalyptic nappy incident might make for a hilarious tweet now, but if it comes to light when they're older, how could it affect the way they feel about themselves, or you, or how others see them? Could their online childhood become an issue if they are seeking a job, or a relationship, or even election to public office?

Your child's right to privacy

Psychologist Aric Sigman has expressed concerned about the impact on children of the eroding boundaries between private and public online: "Part of the way a child forms their identity involves having private information about themselves that remains private."

Parent bloggers

If you've set up a blog to share your parenting experiences with a wider audience, you've probably already given plenty of thought to issues like your child's privacy, managing their digital footprint, ownership and copyright, and commercialism.

Strategies adopted by some successful bloggers include: anonymising their own and their child's identities; involving their child in the material you create and only posting material they are happy with; and carefully monitoring their child's online presence, for example by checking their name in search aggregator services or setting up a Google Alert for their name.

⇨ The above information is reprinted with kind permission from ThinkUKnow. Please visit www. thinkuknow.co.uk for further information.

Key Facts

⇨ Over 100 countries now have some form of privacy and data protection law. (page 2)

⇨ Article 8 protects your right to respect for your private life, your family life, your home and your correspondence (letters, telephone calls and emails, for example). (page 3)

⇨ Every website you visit, the fact of every communication you make, and every mobile app that connects to the internet can now be logged, recorded and made accessible to the Government. (page 6)

⇨ The Investigatory Powers Bill [enhances] the spying powers open to police, intelligence agencies and public bodies and will provide strong legal backing for "bulk" collection (and hacking) of communications. (page 7)

⇨ The first ever legally-binding international treaty dealing with privacy and data protection was the signing of Convention 108 on January 28, 1981 by the Council of Europe. (page 9)

⇨ The newly enforced Investigatory Powers Bill gives 48 government agencies access to your internet connection records; a log of which internet services you've accessed. These include which websites you've visited and even when you've used instant messaging apps. (19)

⇨ The use of CCTV in the UK, and its impact on human rights and civil liberties, regularly hits the headlines. Concerns are raised both about the number of CCTV cameras in the UK and the lack of regulation regarding their use. (page 25)

⇨ Most people (53%) say that, specifically, phone and internet companies should be required to retain everyone's internet browsing history, emails, voice calls, social media interactions, and mobile messaging, which the police and intelligence agencies would be able to access for anti-terrorism purposes. 31% would oppose giving the security forces these powers. (page 27)

⇨ Research conducted in 2002 suggested that there were 4.2 million CCTV cameras in the UK – equating to one CCTV camera for every 14 people. So startling was this statistic that it has been seized upon by critics of CCTV ever since. However, this figure was based on an extrapolation from a survey conducted in one area of London and now seems likely to be unreliable. (page 25)

⇨ The ICO recommends that users of drones – also called unmanned aerial systems (UAS) or unmanned aerial vehicles (UAVs) – with cameras should operate them in a responsible way to respect the privacy of others. (page 30)

⇨ The 'Internet of Things' (IoT) is a term used to describe devices which can connect via the internet and can communicate with us and each other. Used efficiently, these IoT devices could transform the way in which we live, with technology assisting various tasks and processes as we go about our daily lives. (page 31)

⇨ Six in ten 'Internet of Things' devices don't properly tell customers how their personal information is being used, an international study has found. (page 33)

⇨ A recent report showed that:

- 59 per cent of devices failed to adequately explain to customers how their personal information was collected, used and disclosed;

- 68 per cent failed to properly explain how information was stored;

- 72 per cent failed to explain how customers could delete their information off the device and

- 38 per cent failed to include easily identifiable contact details if customers had privacy concerns. (page 33)

⇨ As a newer Internet connected device, smart TVs are less likely to receive proper security support. This is in part because users don't expect them, because of the variety of different operating systems, and as security isn't traditionally the remit of TV manufacturers. Added to this, users are less likely to use best security practices when it comes to their TV, such as changing passwords and regularly updating the software. (page 34)

⇨ A study undertaken in the US by Pew Research found that 91% of 12- to 17-year-olds posted selfies online, 24% posted videos of themselves. Another 91% were happy posting their real name, 82% their birthday, 71% where they live and the school they attend, 53% their email address and 20% their mobile phone number. (page 35)

⇨ Given the exponential growth of reality shows and social media, children now have unprecedented access to the inner thoughts and personal actions of others. Children are growing up watching real people freely share their deep personal ideas, experiences, opinions and actions. (page 36)

⇨ Mattel's latest WiFi enabled Barbie doll can easily be hacked to turn it into a surveillance device for spying on children and listening into conversations without the owner's knowledge. (page 37)

Article 8: Right to privacy

Article 8 of the European Convention on Human Rights states that `Everyone has the right for his private and family life, his home and his correspondence.` There are some exceptions to this rule however, so this means that your right to privacy can be interfered with as long as it is `in accordance with law` and `necessary in a democratic society`.

Big Brother

The term comes from a character in George Orwell`s novel Nineteen Eighty-Four, from which the phrase `Big Brother is watching you` originated. Big Brother embodied totalitarianism; a regime where the government controls and monitors every aspect of people`s lives and behaviour.

Biometric data

Biometrics (or biometric authentication) refers to a method of uniquely identifying people. This includes methods such as fingerprints, DNA, retinal scans (eyes) and facial recognition; something that is permanent throughout a person`s lifetime and doesn`t change as they age. The main uses of biometric data are for the purpose of controlling access (e.g. some laptops have fingerprint scanners) or helping tackle and prevent crime.

CCTV

Closed-circuit television (CCTV) is the use of mounted video cameras which broadcast a live image to a television screen closely watched over by someone (can be recorded). CCTV is used to observe an area in an effort to reduce and prevent crime. However, the use of CCTV has triggered a debate about security versus privacy.

Communication Data Bill

This legislation would mean that Internet service provider (ISP) and mobile phone services would be able to gather much more data about what their customers are doing. Currently, communication monitoring is limited to data such as who people send emails to and who they ring, not the actual content of the messages themselves, for 12 months. This Bill would extend it to webmail, voice calls, social media and Internet gaming. This is why it has been labelled as the `Snooper`s Charter`. It is estimated to cost approximately £1.8 billion.

Data Protection Act 1988 (DPA)

This act exists to protect personal information about people. It ensures that personal data is kept secure, accurate and up-to-date. You can ask to see data about you (the `right of access`), but not other peoples. Other people cannot ask to see data about you. The organisation has up to 40 days to reply to your request. You have the right to know why that data is being held, where the data has come from and if any automated decisions are being made about you using this data.

DNA

DNA stands for deoxyribonucleic acid. It is the genetic material contained in the cells of all living things and it carries the information that allows organisms to function, repair and reproduce themselves. Every cell of plants, micro-organisms (such as bacteria), animals and people contain many thousands of different genes, which are made of DNA. These genes determine the characteristics, or genetic make-up, of every living thing, including the food we eat. When we eat any food, we are eating the genes and breaking down the DNA present in the food.

DNA database/United Kingdom National DNA Database

The UK has a national database of DNA profiles which the police can use to match suspect DNA. Samples are taken from crime scenes, police suspects and anyone arrested and detained at a police station (in England and Wales). The database has helped in solving both past and present crimes. However, controversial privacy issues about the DNA database have arisen because samples have been taken and held onto from people who are innocent and some people feel that they should be removed/destroyed from the database. In March 2012 the database is estimated to contain almost six million individual records.

Protection of Freedoms Act 2012

An act that regulates the use of biometric data, the use of surveillance and many other things. For example, this will mean schools need to get parents` consent before processing child`s biometric information and it also introduces a code of practice for surveillance camera systems. Essentially, this is to help protect people from state intrusion in their lives.

Snooper's Charter (Draft Communications Data Bill)

Draft legislation that would require Internet service providers and mobile phone companies to keep records of their user's Internet search history, emails, calls and texts.

Surveillance

The close observation and monitoring of behaviour or activities. To keep watch over a person or group. The UK has been described as a `surveillance society` because of its large number of CCTV cameras and the national DNA database; the UK was once referred to as `the most surveilled country` in the Western states.

Assignments

Brainstorming

⇨ In small groups, discuss what you know about privacy, in the UK and abroad.

- What is the 'right to privacy'?

- What is CCTV?

- What is The Snooper's Charter?

Research

⇨ Look up the Human Convention, article 8 Right to Privacy. Find out what the Universal Declaration of Human Rights (1948) says about the right to privacy. Can you think of any situations in your own experience where this right has not been observed? You might find Right to a private and family life useful. Discuss in pairs.

⇨ Using a map, create an illustrated diagram comparing and contrasting different worldviews on privacy – what might be law in Great Britain, might be completely different in somewhere like China. See The invention of privacy for further information.

⇨ Research surveillance drones: are they an invasion of privacy or a useful tool for law enforcement and research? Debate this in pairs and feedback to the rest of your class.

⇨ Choose a partner. Using the Internet, research your partner from the perspective of someone who doesn't already know them and note down what you find out about them. You could try typing their name into a search engine and having a look at social media sites such as Facebook or Twitter. How much information have you found? Do you think your partner takes enough care with their online safety? Give them some feedback.

Design

⇨ Choose one of the articles from this book and create an illustration that highlights the key themes of the piece.

⇨ Design a series of posters and web-banners that will advertise Data Privacy Day.

⇨ Design an infographic that demonstrates the key aspects of 'Freedom of Information'.

⇨ Design a piece of wearable technology that a firm could use to track their employees actions. Think about what kind of things employers would want to keep an eye on, e.g. use of work email, amount of time away from desk or Internet use.

⇨ Design a leaflet that explains how to delete yourself and your searches from Google's history.

⇨ Imagine that you work for a group of local volunteers who are campaigning to increase the amount of CCTV in your town. Create a series of posters that could be displayed at bus-stops to raise awareness of your cause.

Oral

⇨ Create a PowerPoint presentation, arguing that smart technology such as Smart TVs are a dangerous step towards invasion of privacy. Share with your class.

⇨ In small groups, think about what you would tell someone who has just started using the Internet about how they should guard their privacy. Make a bullet point list and share with the rest of your class.

⇨ As a class, stage a debate in which one half of you argues that the Snooper's Charter is a necessary and beneficial piece of legislation and the other half argues that it is a breach of people's right to privacy.

⇨ In pairs, discuss how you feel about CCTV surveillance. Is it a good thing? Or an invasion of privacy?

Reading/writing

⇨ Write a short story about what the future would be like if a government who abused technology such as CCTV, ID cards and the DNA database came to power. How might they use these things to control citizens? What would life be like for people living in this future society? Your story should be at least 700 words.

⇨ Write a blog post from the point of view of the Austrian teenager who sued their parents for posting pictures of them on Facebook (see page 38).

⇨ Read the article *Online and out there: how children view privacy differently from adults* and write an article exploring your own opinion on the matter.

⇨ Write a one paragraph definition of the following:

- Privacy

- Surveillance

- The Internet of Things.

⇨ Imagine that your head teacher has decided to start using surveillance drones to keep an eye on what students are doing. Write a letter explaining why you think this would be a gross breach of students' privacy.

Acknowledgements

The publisher is grateful for permission to reproduce the material in this book. While every care has been taken to trace and acknowledge copyright, the publisher tenders its apology for any accidental infringement or where copyright has proved untraceable. The publisher would be pleased to come to a suitable arrangement in any such case with the rightful owner.

Images

All images courtesy of iStock except p.11 © Oliur Rahman, p.16 © Mitchell Hollander, p.19 © Sonia Langford, p.25 © Rishabh Varshney , p.30 © Annie Spratt and p.38 © William Iven.

Icons

Icons on page 12 were made (from top left to bottom right) by Prosymbols, Freepik, Madebyoliver, Prosymbols, Pixel Perfect, Madebyoliver, Madebyoliver, Madebyoliver, IEP, Madebyoliver, Gregor Cresnar and Madebyoliver from www.flaticon.com.

Illustrations

Don Hatcher: pages 14 & 29. Simon Kneebone: pages 5 & 37. Angelo Madrid: pages 1 & 32.

Additional acknowledgements

Editorial on behalf of Independence Educational Publishers by Cara Acred.

With thanks to the Independence team: Mary Chapman, Sandra Dennis, Jackie Staines and Jan Sunderland.

Cara Acred

Cambridge, May 2017